SETTLERS ON THE EASTERN SHORE

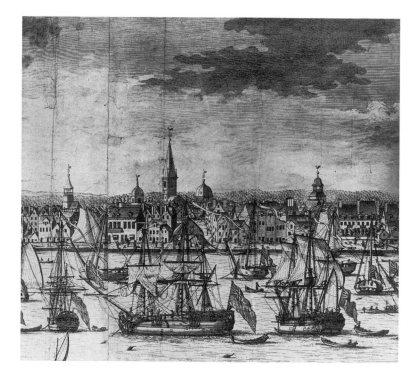

Manhattan in 1716, seen from Brooklyn Heights, with the East River and its shipping in the foreground. From a panorama painted in 1716 by William Burgis. (Library of Congress)

The Library of American History
General Editor: John Anthony Scott

SETTLERS ON THE EASTERN SHORE

The British Colonies in
North America
1607–1750

John Anthony Scott

Illustrated with contemporary
prints and photographs

Facts On File
New York • Oxford

Facts On File, Inc.   Facts On File Limited
460 Park Avenue South   Collins Street
New York NY 10016   Oxford OX4 1XJ
USA   United Kingdom

Scott, John Anthony, 1916–
    Settlers on the Eastern Shore, 1607–1750 / John Anthony Scott.
      p. cm.
    Includes bibliographical references (p.) and index.
    Summary: Selections from original accounts of life in early
settlements, linked by the editor's historical narrative, show the
hardship and hope of servant, slave, and settler in early America.
    ISBN 0-8160-2327-1
    1. Unite States—History—Colonial period, ca. 1600–1775.
    [1. United States—History—Colonial period, ca. 1600–1775.]
    Title.
    E188.S36   1991
    973.2—dc20   90-13860

A British CIP catalogue record for this book is available from the
British Library.

Facts On File books are available at special discounts when
purchased in bulk quantities for businesses, associations,
institutions or sales promotions. Please call our Special Sales
Department in New York at 212/683-2244 (dial 800/322-8755 except
in NY, AK, or HI) or in Oxford at 865/728399.

Text Design by Donna Sinisgalli
Jacket Design by Solonay/Mitchell Associates
Composition by Facts On File Inc.
Manufactured by The Maple-Vail Book Manufacturing Group
Printed in the United States of America
Maps reproduced by special arrangement with Alfred A. Knopf, Inc.

10 9 8 7 6 5 4 3 2 1

This book is printed on acid-free paper.

For Maria

CONTENTS

PREFACE

Millions of American young people passing through our schools and colleges learn their United States history almost exclusively from standard textbooks. Growing dissatisfaction with these texts was eloquently voiced when Frances Fitzgerald published *America Revised: History Schoolbooks in the Twentieth Century* in 1979. High school history texts, Fitzgerald charged, are supremely dull and uninteresting. They fail to hold the attention of young people or to fire their imagination. United States history ought to arouse wonder, compassion and delight, but these books turn it into a crashing bore. One of the reasons for this, she said, is that the texts do not often draw upon the marvelous original sources that this nation inherits, which constitute the lifeblood of history, and which are indispensable to its study, no matter what the age of the student.

Efforts to find alternatives to the traditional texts began some years before Fitzgerald's book appeared. One of these was an initiative that Alfred A. Knopf launched in 1966. The result was the publication, during the years 1967–77, of an historical series designed for the use of high school students and of undergraduates and entitled The Living History Library. In all, fifteen volumes were published in this series. Each book was written by a distinguished historian or teacher. Each told the story of a different period or topic in American history—the colonial period, the American Revolution, the black experience in the Civil

War, the cowboy in the West, the Great Depression and so on. Each was based upon original sources woven throughout into the framework of the narrative. Ordinary people who witnessed historical events and participated in historical struggles provided their own testimony and told their own story both in word and song. The series presented the American experience through the medium of a new literary art form. People long dead and struggles long past came to life again in the present.

The historical and literary value of the books has not diminished with the passage of time. On the contrary, the need for books such as these is greater today than it has ever been before. Innumerable important topics in our history await treatment of this type. Facts On File is happy to publish new and updated editions of the Living History Library books as part of its Library of American History.

Scattered tribes of Indians inhabited the eastern shore of North America. They lived a free life, fishing, hunting, gathering food and cultivating corn and vegetables in the forest clearings. White colonists coming in killed the Indians or drove them away, cleared the forests and planted farms. Wealthier farmers imported white servants to work for them, but in many places and especially the south, these were never enough. Africans, kidnapped in their own native land, were brought over here in chains to fill the gap. Whether rich or poor, most of the white colonists were linked to the motherland by the ties of a common culture and were proud to call themselves British. During the years of the colonial era to 1750 they fashioned an economic, political and social structure as the foundations for a new and independent American civilization.

1

WANDERERS IN EDEN

And the Lord God planted a garden eastward in Eden;
and there he put the man whom he had formed.

Genesis

America, as it was to be settled by colonists from the British Isles and Western Europe, was the long strip of rocky shore and coastal plain that lay between the Appalachian Mountains on the west and the Atlantic Ocean on the east, between the forests of Maine and New Brunswick on the north and the wilds of Georgia on the south. From 1607 to 1750, European settlers occupied this territory and made it their home; in the course of so doing, they became Americans, living in a new land that would be the source of their livelihood, the scene of their struggles, the object of their love. This book tells their story.

The people who came to America in the 16th and 17th centuries—geographers, explorers, fishermen, sea captains and settlers—discovered a country of unbelievable variety and beauty; nature, here, lay before their wondering eyes on a stupendous scale. Wildlife flourished with luxuriant fertility. We might think that the descriptions of the New World that many of these people wrote were impudent exaggerations, if it were not for the fact that so many of them agreed on so many points.

Colonial America, except where the Indians had cleared the land and were cultivating it, or where natural meadows existed, was an unbroken wilderness of tall, ancient and stately trees of many varieties. As an unknown author wrote in a promotional pamphlet of 1666, *A Brief Description of the Province of Carolina*:

> *The whole country consists of stately woods, groves, marshes, and meadows; it abounds with variety of as brave oak as eye can behold, great bodies tall and straight from 60 to 80 feet before there be any boughs, which with the little underwood makes the woods very commodious to travel in, either on horseback or afoot. In the barren sandy ground grow most stately pines, white and red cedars, ash, birch, holly, chestnut and walnut trees of great growth and very plentiful.*

Wild fruits grew in abundance throughout the land and by the waters of its endless streams. One traveler, the Reverend Johannes Megapolensis, described the region around Albany, New York in 1644. He wrote that the hills were covered with blueberry bushes; wild strawberries grew so thick in the river meadows that a man might lie down among them and eat his fill. Grapevines, too, flourished along the roads, trails and creeks. Robert Beverley who wrote the first history of Virginia, wrote that the Indian cherry grew on small slender trees so heavy with fruit that they were "scarce able to support themselves." The early settlers, too, spoke of many other fruits that grew in profusion in the woods and fields—peaches, cranberries, gooseberries and plums.

British America teemed with wildfowl. When they took wing, the flocks were of such stupendous size that the earth was darkened by their passage. Captain Arthur Barlowe, who landed on the coast of North Carolina in 1584, described how "great flocks of cranes arose: their cries were multiplied by many echoes; they made a noise as if an army shouted all together." John Smith, one of the founders of Virginia, wrote in 1612 about the country's great variety of birds: eagles, hawks, partridges, wild turkeys, red-winged blackbirds, thrushes and many more. In the winter, he said, "there are a great plenty of swans, cranes grey and white with black wing, herons, geese, brants, duck, parrots and pigeons."

American rivers, lakes and shores teemed with fish. Reverend Thomas Higginson, who settled in Massachusetts, wrote in 1630 that "the abundance of sea fish is almost beyond believing and sure I should scarce have believed it except I had seen it with my own eyes." Robert Beverley told how the herring in Virginia came up the rivers to spawn in the spring in such abundance that "it is almost impossible to ride through [the fords] without treading on them." "Thus," he said, "do those poor creatures expose their own lives to some hazard, out of a care to find a more convenient reception for their young, which are not yet alive."

John Lederer left a remarkable record of the animals that inhabited the American forest. Lederer was a young German scientist who explored the Virginia uplands and the Blue Ridge Mountains in 1660. He prepared carefully for his travels in these uncharted lands. He took with him a compass, and axes to fell trees and bridge rivers. A party of Indians accompanied him to blaze trails and to build lean-tos for shelter on the way. A horse, a gun, Indian corn, blankets and a hammock completed his equipment.

Lederer noted that the thickets harbored all sorts of beasts of prey like wolves, panthers, bears and wild hogs; also small mammals such as wildcats, foxes and raccoons. He saw herds of deer roaming the woods and grasslands in countless numbers. "Beaver and otter," he wrote, "I met with at every river that I passed."

Lederer particularly described the American wildcat that preyed on the deer. The wildcat, he wrote "is something bigger than our English fox, of a reddish grey color, and in everyway agreeing with an ordinary cat; fierce, ravenous and cunning: for finding the deer, upon which they delight to prey, too swift for them, they watch upon branches of trees, and as [the deer] walk or feed under, jump down upon them."

There were dangers lurking in the woods. Observers from New England to Georgia commented on "...serpents called rattlesnakes that have rattles in their tails, that will not fly from a man as others will, but will fly upon him and sting him so mortally that he will die within a quarter of an hour after." By all accounts these rattlesnakes were of formidable size. Lederer recounts how he met with one "...of an extraordinary length and thickness, for I judged it two yards and a half or better from head to tail, and as big about as a man's arm." He killed the snake and opened it, finding, to his astonishment, that the reptile had swallowed a small squirrel. "Which caused in me," he said, "a double wonder: first, how such a reptile should catch so nimble a creature as a squirrel; and having caught it, how she could swallow it entire."

Robert Beverley agreed with Higginson, Lederer and others that the rattlesnake was a dangerous creature, but he felt that this danger had been exaggerated. "For in the first place," he wrote, "this snake is very rarely seen; and when that happens, it never does the least mischief, unless you offer to disturb it, and thereby provoke it to bite in its own defense. But it never fails to give you fair warning, by making a noise with its rattle, which may be heard at a convenient distance."

Much less dangerous than rattlesnakes, thought Beverley, but far more bothersome, were the mosquitoes. "They are," he said, "a long-tailed gnat, such as are in all fens and low ground in England, and, I think, have no other difference than the name." The American gnats, he thought, were more vicious than the English ones as a result of the hot sun, which gave them a longer season in which to breed and bother people.

North America, with its lofty hills, verdant water meadows, its shining, unpolluted streams, its carpets of flowers, was the home of the Indian peoples. The Indians, scattered across the length and breadth of the continent, had inhabited North America for thousands of years before the coming of the white man. The early European settlers, explorers and missionaries observed these early Americans with the same freshness, the same sense of wonder, that the beauty and the glory of the New World itself inspired.

The great majority of the Indians who lived in what is now the United States existed at the *neolithic* culture level. They were ignorant, that is, of the use of metals like copper, bronze, iron, or steel. The tools on which they depended for the cultivation of the earth, for hunting and for making war were fashioned out of stone or bone.

When the whites arrived, many tribes and bands of these neolithic people were scattered throughout the forests of the eastern seaboard. They lived in villages amid the forest clearings, following a way of life that was partly nomadic, or wandering, and partly settled. In the warm weather, they planted squash, beans and corn, cultivated them in the gardens around their homes and stored much of the harvest for winter use; they fished, in the rivers and along the shores; they gathered berries, roots, nuts and oysters. When winter approached and the weather turned cold, they took to the woods and hunted bear, elk and deer. Much of the gardening work, as well as taking care of the children, making clothes and cooking, was left to the women. The men did the hunting and fishing, manufactured weapons and tools—at which they showed an extraordinary ingenuity—and, when necessary, went to war. The Indians held their hunting lands and gardens in common, were closely bound to each other by ties of kinship and a common life, and adored their children. They were the first American patriots. They crossed the land on moccasined feet and worshipped America as the mother and giver of life. The splendor of their country found expression in the names that they gave to its rivers, lakes, mountains and forests.

The Indians practiced the same hunting, fishing, gathering and gardening economy throughout the colonial area, but the different groups showed great variety in terms of patterns of life, language and belief. Their fine physique and appearance aroused the admiration of observers. Speaking, for example, of the Mohawk people at Albany in 1644, Reverend Megapolensis described them as having "well formed features, bodies and limbs; they all have black hair and eyes, but their skin is yellow." In summer they wore little or no clothing; in the winter they wrapped themselves in bear or deer skins, or made themselves garments out of the skins of smaller animals like beaver, otter, or squirrel, which they sewed together. "The women as well as the men," he said, "go with their heads bare. The women let their hair grow very long, and tie it

*The Indian town of Pomeiock as it looked to the artist John White, who sailed with Britain's first colonizing venture to Roanoke, Virginia in 1585.
Engraved from White's original watercolor by Theodore de Bry.* (Library of Congress)

together a little, and let it hang down their backs." As for the men, most wore their hair short in a broad close-cropped band running from the forehead all the way across the top of the head down to the neck. The hair stood, said Megapolensis, "right on end like a cock's comb or hog's bristles."

All Indian weapons and tools—bows and arrows, needles, hatchets and knives—had to be made of bone, stone or wood, since the people did not know the use of copper, iron or steel. For planting seed and cultivating crops, they used a variety of hoes and digging sticks. "The Indians," wrote Jacques Le Moyne, a French artist who visited Florida in 1564, "till the soil very diligently, using a kind of hoe made from fish bone fitted to wooden handles. Since the soil is light, these serve well enough to cultivate it." He also noted the interesting fact that after the ground had been broken up and leveled "the planting is done by women, some making holes with sticks, into which others drop seeds of bean and maize."

Thomas Hariot, who explored the Virginia coast in 1585, has left a vivid picture of the Indian method of fishing. "They have," he wrote, "a remarkable way of fishing in their rivers. As they have neither steel nor iron, they fasten the sharp, hollow tail of a certain fish (something like a sea crab) to reeds or to the end of a long rod, and with this point they spear the fish both by day and night."

Hariot was impressed by the simplicity of Indian life and its joy. "It is a pleasing picture," he said, "to see these people wading and sailing in their shallow rivers. They are untroubled by the desire to pile up riches for their children and they live in perfect contentment with their present state, in friendship with each other, sharing those things with which God has so plentifully provided them."

The Indian joy of life was also expressed in the love of play. Indian games were fun, and they also helped young men and women harden their bodies and perfect their hunting skills. "The young men," said Le Moyne, "are trained to run races, and a prize is given to the one who shows the greatest endurance in the contest. They also practice a great deal with bow and arrow."

Le Moyne has left a description of the way in which Florida Indians hunted the deer with these weapons. "They hide themselves," he wrote, "in the skin of a very large deer which they have killed some time before. They place the animal's head upon their own head, looking through the eye holes as through a mask." With this ingenious camouflage, the hunters were able to approach the deer without frightening them into flight and were then able to draw their bows and kill them with well-aimed arrows.

The Indians not only wandered through the forest in search of game, but they built boats so seaworthy that they could travel many miles up the American rivers and out to the islands fringing the mainland shores. "The way they build their boats," wrote Thomas Hariot, "is very wonderful. For although they completely lack any iron tools such as we use, they can make boats as good as ours. And these boats are seaworthy enough to take them sailing or fishing wherever they want to go." Hariot described how the Indians, with no other aid but fire and seashells, made these ocean-going craft:

First they choose a tall, thick tree of the size required for the boat's frame. Then they light a fire close to its roots, feeding it bit by bit with dry moss and small chips of wood, keeping the flames from mounting too high. When the tree is almost burnt through, they make a good fire to cause it to fall. Then they burn off the tops and boughs, taking care that the trunk should not be shortened.

The tree is raised on a platform built on forked posts at a height convenient for working. The bark is stripped off with sharp shells; the inner length of the trunk is kept for the bottom of the boat. A fire is made all along the length of the trunk, and when it has burned sufficiently it is quenched and the charred wood scraped away with shells. Then they build a new fire, burn out another piece, and so on, sometimes burning and sometimes scraping, until the boat has a good bottom.

Indian families enjoyed little that they might call their own: a few sleeping mats or blankets, a few wooden dishes

and baskets, hatchets, tobacco pipes and hunting implements would make up the store of a family's wealth.
Houses were a variety of sizes and shapes, and several
families might live under the shelter of the same roof. The
huts, as Thomas Higginson described them, were "...little
and homely, being made with small poles pricked [pushed]
into the ground; and so bent and fastened at the tops and
on the sides, they are matted with boughs and covered on
the roof with sedge and old mats." A collection of huts,
forming a village, often as not would be palisaded with
high wooden stakes as a protection from wild animals and
surprise attack.

Such, in brief, was the land and the people the Europeans, found when, in the 17th century, they sailed across
the Atlantic to colonize the New World. How, in less than
150 years, they took over this paradise and laid the foundations of a new society is the story that will unfold in the
chapters that follow.

2

THE WEATHERBEATEN SHORE:
Early Settlers in New England

Get thee out of thy country, and from thy kindred, and from thy father's house, unto a land that I will show thee: and I will make of thee a great nation, and I will bless thee, and make thy name great.

Genesis

Many of the first colonists who crossed the Atlantic in the 17th century came to New England. They were Puritans or Separatists fleeing from persecution by the king of England and from the established forms of belief and worship in the Old Country. Puritans were members of the Church of England who wished to return to the simplicity of Christian life and fellowship that existed many centuries before in the earliest days of the Christian church. They wished to *purify* the English church of its false beliefs, its paintings and its idols, its stained glass, its overpaid officials. Separatists went one step further: they believed in *separating* themselves from the established church and forming new, independent groups of believers.

To the 17th century religious reformer, whether a Puritan or Separatist, the word of God had to be sought in the Bible alone, not in the teaching of priests or the laws of

churches. These reformers—we may also call them Protestants, for the words are interchangeable—felt close in
spirit to the Jews of old; they studied with care the tales
of Jewish bondage and of the flight from Egyptian oppression that were unfolded in the Old Testament—in Genesis,
Exodus, Numbers, Leviticus and Joshua. The Puritans
and Separatists felt that they, even as the Jews of old,
must take flight from bondage in England.

The Jews, they reasoned, had fled from Pharaoh and his
taskmasters. Puritans and Separatists must flee from
Charles I, king of England, his church and his servants.
The Jews had gone out into the wilderness; they had
braved the desert wastes in their search for the Promised
Land. Puritans and Separatists, too, must brave the
wastes—the wild wastes of the Atlantic seas. Beyond,
crossing by the grace of God and under His providence or
protection, they would find the promised land, America,
promised to them even as Jerusalem was promised to the
Children of Israel.

The early settlers of New England had a deep conviction
that suffering, sacrifice and death in the New World were
preferable to persecution in the Old World. This made the
New England settlements unique; most of the other settlements owed their origin to quite different motives. This
New England faith would set its stamp on American life
throughout years to come.

Many years before the first permanent settlements
were made, the weatherbeaten shores of New England had
become well-known to English seafarers for their wealth
of fish. That tough English mariner, John Smith, one of
the founders of Virginia, wrote in his *Description of New
England* in 1616 that "in various sandy bays a man may
draw with a net great store of mulletts, basses, and various
other sorts of excellent fish, as many as his net can draw
on shore." Thus when the settlers came to Plymouth in the
Mayflower in 1620, they landed in an area quite well-
known to their countrymen. The story is best told in the
words of William Bradford, the plantation's second governor.

Bradford's *Of Plymouth Plantation* is one of the most
famous books in American history. The manuscript lay

around gathering dust until it was finally discovered and published in 1856, exactly 200 years after its author's death. The writing is beautiful. In Bradford's words, the much-told tale has a freshness that cannot be lost.

William Bradford was a Protestant, a farmer and a member of a Separatist group at Scrooby, Nottinghamshire, in the north of England. Religious persecution under King James I made life intolerable for the young man and his friends. "They could not continue long," he wrote, "in any peaceable condition, but were hunted and persecuted on every side...For some were taken and clapped in prison, others had their houses beset and watched night and day...and most were forced to flee and leave their houses and habitations, and the means of their livelihood."

These Separatists fled first of all to the Netherlands. Holland was a Protestant country, which in 1608—when the Separatists emigrated there from England—was just emerging from a long bloody struggle with Spain for its independence. Sadly, the Separatist band made its way to the port of Boston in Lincolnshire and sailed into exile, "to go into a country," as Bradford wrote, "where they must learn a new language and get their living they knew not how."

The exiles settled in the town of Leyden. There they stayed for a few years, earning their living as clothmakers and "enjoying much sweet and delightful society and spiritual comfort together in the ways of God."

But Bradford and his friends realized that they could not stay in Leyden for good. Life there was hard, so that some of them went back to their native land, choosing, as he said, "the prisons of England rather than this liberty in Holland, with these afflictions." Old age and death further diminished the band; worst of all, the young people began to drift away from the English community and to forget the faith of their fathers and mothers. Many of the youth, wrote Bradford, "were oftentimes so oppressed with their heavy labor that though their minds were free and willing, yet their bodies bowed under the weight of the same, and became decrepit in their early youth, the vigor of nature being consumed in the very bud, as it were." Even more tragic for the parents was to see their children lured away by evil example, taking up soldiering as a profession and abandoning their homes.

To preserve their community and their families, the Separatists began to debate whether they should immigrate to America. "The place they had thought on," wrote Bradford, "was some of those vast and unpeopled countries of America which are fruitful and fit for habitation, being devoid of all civil inhabitants, where there are only savage and brutish men which range up and down, little otherwise than the wild beasts."

Some urged emigration. Others, more cautious, warned that many hazards were involved, like the perils of the sea and the length of the voyage, which old people and women would never be able to endure. Beyond that, they said, "the miseries of the land...would be too hard to be borne and [would be] likely to consume and utterly ruin them." They would be exposed to famine, nakedness and want; they would fall victim to fatal diseases. Even if they escaped all these, they would still be "in continual danger of the savage people, who are cruel, barbarous, and most treacherous, being furious in their rage and merciless when they overcome."

Others answered, certainly there would be difficulties and dangers. The important thing was to face these with courage and resolution. These dangers, said they, "were great, but not desperate. The difficulties were many, but not invincible."

So the debate raged on. In the end some decided to stay but most decided to go. When everything was ready they boarded their ship the *Mayflower*, and said their farewells. It was, wrote Bradford, very sad "to see what sighs and sobs and prayers did sound amongst them, what tears did gush from every eye."

The Pilgrims sailed across the Atlantic for nine long weeks. Their destination was the Hudson River, but stormy weather obliged them to cast anchor off Cape Cod. William Bradford recorded the scene. "Being thus arrived in a good harbor," he wrote, "and brought safe to land, they fell upon their knees and blessed the God of Heaven who had brought them over the vast and furious ocean, and delivered them from all the perils and miseries thereof, again to set their feet on the firm and stable earth."

It was November 1620. Ahead was the winter wilderness; in back, the wild sea's wastes. Bradford wrote:

And for the season it was winter, and they that know the winters of that country know them to be sharp and violent and subject to cruel and fierce storms, dangerous to travel to known places, much more to search an unknown coast. Besides, what could they see but a hideous and desolate wilderness, full of wild beasts and wild men—and what multitudes there might be of them they knew not. Neither could they, as it were, go up to the top of Pisgah to view from this wilderness a more goodly country to feed their hopes; for which way soever they turned their eyes (save upward to the heavens) they could have little solace or content in respect of any outward objects. For summer being done, all things stand upon them with a weatherbeaten face, and the whole country, full of woods and thickets, represented a wild and savage hue. If they looked behind them, there was the mighty ocean which they had passed and was now as a main bar and gulf to separate them from all the civil parts of the world.

The settlers did not despair. Landing at Plymouth, they set to work unloading their stores from the ship and building cottages; during the winter many died, but in the spring the survivors planted corn, caught fish and shot turkeys and waterfowl. Within a few years, the colony was firmly established.

The Plymouth colony was a lasting symbol of pioneer courage in the face of seemingly insurmountable obstacles; but in the settlement of Massachusetts, it played a minor role and lived on, as it were, in a backwater. The main thrust of colonization in New England came with settlers who began to arrive in large numbers in the Boston area 10 years later in 1630.

One of the best introductions to them that we have is a letter their leader, Thomas Dudley, wrote from Boston in 1631 to a friend in the Old World. Thomas Dudley was one of a number of Puritans who came together to organize the immigration to the New World, and who, in 1629, secured from King Charles I a charter, or permission, to undertake a trading venture to be called the Massachusetts Bay Company. This charter was to be a very important legal document. The state of Massachusetts, in the course of time, would emerge from the company that it set up.

In those days of great ocean voyages, explorers laid claim to lands that they discovered on behalf of the countries from which they came. They planted their own flags on foreign soil; they took possession of foreign lands in the name of their own kings. Thus the kings of England came to feel that they were the legal owners of America by virtue of the explorations of British seafarers. They began to give charters to groups and individuals; they gave, in these charters, title to land in their overseas territories, permission to trade there, authority to set up government. All the American colonies owed their legal existence to such charters. These were, in a very real sense, the original constitutions of the United States.

The royal charters were written in quaint, long-winded legal language. In the charter of the Massachusetts Bay Company, the group was given title to "all that part of New England in America which lies...between a great river there, commonly called Merrimac River, and a certain other river there, called Charles River..."

In return for this generous grant, the Massachusetts Bay Company undertook to pay the crown a fifth part of all the gold and silver that might be found on any of the company's lands. Under the charter, too, the company and its settlers in the area would enjoy "free liberty of fishing" in the rivers that flowed through their settlement, and in the ocean that washed its shores.

The charter also granted to the company the right to govern the Massachusetts Bay Colony in the name of the king. Stating that a prosperous colony, or "plantation," could not develop without government and order, it authorized the company to establish itself as "a body corporate and politic," or a government composed of a governor, deputy governors and 18 assistants. The board thus set up would both direct the affairs of the company and govern the colony. The board, sitting as a "general court," or assembly, was authorized "to make laws for the good and welfare of the said company, and for the government and ordering of the said lands and plantation, and the people inhabiting and to inhabit the same." The important proviso, or condition, was added, that "such laws and ordinances must not be repugnant to the laws and statutes of this our realm of England." This phrase reserved to the king the right to annul, or veto, such colonial laws as did not meet with his approval.

The company was also given permission to recruit settlers in England and to ship them out to Massachusetts; or, as the king put it, "to take, lead, carry and transport...all such and so many of our loving subjects as shall willingly accompany them." Full and absolute authority was also granted "to correct, punish, pardon, govern, and rule all such the subjects of us, our heirs and successors, as shall from time to time adventure themselves." The leaders of the Massachusetts Bay Company, evidently, could govern their settlement pretty much as they pleased.

The Massachusetts Bay Company's venture got under way in 1630, when a fleet of 17 ships was sent out from England. Among those who came in this convoy was Thomas Dudley, the company's first governor. As soon as he could, busy as he was with his numerous duties in the colony when he landed, he sat down and wrote to his dear friend Bridget, countess of Lincoln. He wished to assure her that he had arrived safely and to give her all the news. We must picture him sitting in the winter evening in his tiny cottage in Boston. He wrote as best he could by the light of the flickering wood fire, with the paper on his knee.

Dudley first apologized for the crudeness of the letters that he was scrawling and the rambling quality of his story, "having yet," as he said, "no table, no other room to write in, than by the fireside upon my knee, in this sharp winter." Members of his family were gathered around the fire too, and their conversation constantly distracted him and made him many times, as he told the countess, "forget what I would say, and say what I would not."

Dudley was mindful that he and his companions were not the first English Protestants to land on New England shores and settle there. He recounted briefly the story of the Pilgrims. "About the year 1620," he wrote, "certain English set out from Leyden in Holland intending their course for Hudson's river...These being much weatherbeaten and wearied with seeking the river, after a most tedious voyage arrived at length in a small bay lying north-east from Cape Cod." Landing about the month of December they began to settle at New Plymouth. "After much sickness, famine, poverty and great mortality...they are now grown up to a people, healthy, wealthy, politic and religious."

Yes, as Thomas Dudley looked back on the experience of the Plymouth Separatists, he might well have found comfort and inspiration in their example. For had they not faced the same obstacles—cold, hunger, sickness and despair—that the Bostonians were facing? And had they not persevered and triumphed, with the help of God, over hardship? Should Dudley then fail where Bradford had succeeded? He threw another log on the fire and resumed writing in the light of the flames that licked up around it.

"Touching the plantation which we have here begun," he wrote, "these seventeen ships arrived all safe in New England this year 1630, but made a long, troublesome and a costly voyage being all wind-bound long in England, and hindered with contrary winds after they set sail, and so scattered with mists and tempests that few of them arrived together." Soon, however, settlements began to spring up on both sides of the Charles River—at Charlestown, Boston, Medford, Watertown, Rocksbury, Salem and Dorchester. The work was hard; there was fever and sickness, and many died. "It may be said of us," he wrote sadly, "almost as of the Egyptians, that there is not a house where there is not one dead, and in some houses many."

As time went by, the Boston Bay settlements became established even as Plymouth had and began to spread. Between 1630 and 1650, immigrants arrived in large numbers. New townships were laid out, and the land was divided and allotted to different families for their individual use. Part of each town's lands were set aside for use by everybody—these were common lands, or the town commons. Here all the villagers were entitled to graze their

*This painting of a New England woman and child
was made in the early 1670s by an unknown Boston
artist. The picture has the wooden quality of early colonial art but is valuable for the idea that it conveys
of a colonial woman's costume. The artist had trouble with the baby, which is shown not so much a
child as a miniature adult.* (Worcester Art Museum,
Worcester, Massachusetts)

cattle, sheep and hogs. These animals, of course, the settlers brought over with them in their ships.

In every town community, the people had much business to transact with each other. Therefore they constructed meeting houses that served two purposes. They were forums where the affairs of the community might be discussed and regulations might be passed; they were places of worship where services might be held on the Sabbath or other days.

The meetinghouse was a hall, usually built of wood, large enough to house all the people in the community—farmers, village craftsmen, and servants employed in the home or the field. Usually, the meetinghouse was whitewashed inside and out and furnished with benches or pews where each family had its assigned place. A bell tower or spire topped the structure, so that the community could be "rung in" to a meeting, or an alarm sounded. As the years went by, these buildings became larger and loftier. Bigger windows let in the light of day; tall, wooden pillars graced the covered entrance or portico. Inside, rear and side galleries were added to house larger congregations.

When the English settlers first arrived in New England, they had to find whatever rude shelter they could. Sometimes they copied the Indians and built wigwams framed with saplings and covered with bark, Indian mats or sedge; sometimes they dug crude holes or cellars in the ground and covered them with thatch or turf; and sometimes they simply took refuge in caves. Gradually, as skilled crafts became available, the colonists began to build frame houses—simple one-room affairs at first but enlarged as time and opportunity permitted and sheathed on the outside with clapboards for protection against the bitter winter weather. Chimneys were made of wood, and the roofs covered with a thatch of straw; this was frequently a cause of fire. Governor Dudley reported in 1631 that not only had English wigwams gone up in flames but houses too, "the fire," as he said, "always beginning in the wooden chimneys."

The furnishings of these early farmhouses were simple: a few wooden stools, benches, tables and bedsteads; some pewter or wooden plates, spoons and mugs; a fireplace equipped with brick oven, iron tongs, pots, ladles and kettles. Most of these things, particularly if they were made of iron or other metal, had to be brought from England, along with clothes, bedding, farm tools, axes and firearms.

With the passage of time, the variety of clothing and furnishings available to the New Englander greatly increased. The settlers were not slow to realize that their main wealth lay in harvesting the herring and the cod; the shipbuilding business sprang up in a dozen centers, and a fishing fleet was built. Ocean-going vessels began to carry New England fish and lumber to the West Indies and to import both necessities and luxuries from England. Boston, with its crooked streets and crowded wharves, emerged as America's first and, for a long time, most important commercial center.

As Massachusetts thrived and grew, new settlers arrived, thrusting always outward into the wilderness to the north, the south and the west, taking up new lands, founding new towns and arousing the hatred of the Indians who found themselves dispossessed and driven back.

3

THE CAPTIVITY OF MARY ROWLANDSON

Cain talked with Abel his brother: and it came to pass,
when they were in the field that Cain rose up against
Abel his brother, and slew him. And the Lord said
unto Cain, "Where is Abel thy brother?" And he said "I
know not: am I my brother's keeper?" The Lord said,
"What hast thou done? The voice of thy brother's blood
crieth to me from the ground."

Genesis

New England's Indian population was never very large during the 17th century; fairly reliable estimates place it, at least during the earlier years, at about 20,000. Various tribes—the Massachusetts, Narraganset, Pennacook, Mohegan and Pequod—were scattered loosely throughout the forests or clustered along the river valleys and the shores.

The New England Indians were, at first, friendly enough to the white strangers. William Bradford, for example, related how in 1620 the Indian Samoset had been helpful to the Plymouth settlers "in acquainting them with many things concerning the state of the country...as also of the [Indian] people here, of their names, number and strength, of their situation and distance from this place, and who was chief among them."

Samoset and his friends introduced the settlers to Massasoit, chief of the Wampanoags, who inhabited the eastern shores of Narragansett Bay. After what Bradford described as "friendly entertainment" and the giving of gifts, the two sides made an agreement with each other to live in peace and settle their disputes amicably.

These friendly relationships began to be undermined as Europeans arrived in greater numbers, demanding and obtaining portions of the Indian lands for their own use. The first major conflict was the Pequod War of 1637. The Pequods were an eastern Connecticut tribe militantly opposed to white expansion. They fought against the settlers by themselves, without allies. They were crushed and exterminated.

The other Indian tribes were quiet for nearly 40 years after this war. But the advance of white settlement and of Puritan rule was remorseless; this produced, inevitably, a fresh explosion. The new conflict, which broke out in 1675, was called King Philip's War, after Philip, chief of the Wampanoags, who headed the resistance.

Philip was the son of chief Massasoit who, as was mentioned, concluded a treaty with the Plymouth settlers and strove to live at peace with the whites until his death in 1661. Philip's brother, Alexander, then became the new chief; both young men were burning with anger at the wrongs that the whites were inflicting on their people. When Alexander died in 1662 on his way back from Plymouth, Philip became chief. Foreseeing that struggle with the whites was inevitable, Philip sought to unite all the tribes of southern New England so that they might offer a collective resistance—but without success. He was able to win the support only of the Narragansets of Rhode Island, and of the Nipmucks, who were scattered across a huge tract of forest in central Massachusetts between the eastern settlements on the one side and the Connecticut River on the other.

The war began in June 1675. All along the Massachusetts frontier, and up and down the Connecticut River valley, Indians took to the warpath, burning, scalping and slaying. The colonists had come to dread what they called the "bloody insolency" of Indian fighting, when small bands, appearing out of nowhere, descended on frontier settlements, firing the houses and killing the inhabitants.

The Nipmuck attack on Lancaster, Massachusetts was typical of this bloody insolency. On February 10, 1676, a party descended on the town, killed 50 whites and carried off the pastor's wife, Mary Rowlandson. With her, they took three of her children.

Mrs. Rowlandson lived with the Indians as their captive for three months in the freezing New England winter. She has left us a vivid account of her sojourn in the forest and the hardships she endured until she was ransomed and reunited with her husband. Her *Narrative* was first published in 1682. A significant document in colonial history, it reveals what women and children might expect to face on the frontier; it shows the faith of a Puritan mother and the courage she showed; it tells us, too, of the sufferings of the Indians and the determination with which they resisted the white invader.

Mrs. Rowlandson told first of the horror of a surprise attack at dawn. "On the tenth of February," she wrote,"came the Indians with great numbers upon Lancaster. Their first coming was about sun-rising; hearing the noises of some guns, we looked out; several houses were burning, and the smoke ascending to heaven. There were five persons in one house; the father and the mother and a sucking child they knocked on the head, the other two they took and carried away." Other settlers, being caught in the open, were running for their lives. One of them escaped; others were knocked on the head and killed.

Very soon, Mrs. Rowlandson's home was attacked. "The house," she wrote, "stood upon the edge of a hill; some of the Indians got behind the hill, others into the barn, and others behind anything that could shelter them; from all which places they shot against the house, so that the bullets seemed to fly like hail."

Continuing their siege for about two hours, the Indians finally succeeded in setting the house on fire. "Now," she wrote, "is the dreadful hour come, that I have often heard of...but now mine eyes see it. Some in our house were fighting for their lives, others wallowing in their blood, the house on fire over our heads, and the bloody heathen ready to knock us on the head, if we stirred out."

Taking her children by the hand Mrs. Rowlandson tried to leave her home. When they reached the door, a hail of bullets greeted them. They drew back in terror, but as the fire continued to blaze fiercely, there was no choice but to go out and face the Indians in the open. Scenes of horror ensued. Men, women and children were dragged this way and that, scalped, stripped and stabbed. Among the victims was Mary's older sister Elizabeth. Standing in the doorway, Elizabeth contemplated the dreadful scene. "Lord, let me die with them," she exclaimed. The words were hardly out of her mouth when a bullet struck her and she fell lifeless across the threshold.

Mrs. Rowlandson was taken captive. The Indians told her that she would not be harmed if she would go with them, and she consented; captivity, at that moment, seemed a less fearful fate than death. "I had often before this," she wrote, "said that if the Indians should come, I should choose rather to be killed by them than be taken alive. But when it came to the trial my mind changed; their glittering weapons so daunted my spirit, that I chose rather to go along with those, as I may say, ravenous beasts than that moment to end my days."

Both Mary and her six-year-old daughter had been wounded by bullets. She left Lancaster carrying the moaning, dying child in her arms.

The first night was passed on a hill near the town, where the Indians spent the time in dancing, singing and feasting. The next day, they took their leave of Lancaster, taking Mary Rowlandson with them. "I must turn my back upon the town," she wrote, "and travel with them into the vast and desolate wilderness, I knew not whither. It is not my tongue or pen can express the sorrows of my heart and the bitterness of my spirit, that I had at this departure." As for Mary's wounded daughter, the Indians placed the child on a horse. As they led her along, she was moaning "I shall die! I shall die!" Mary followed on foot "with sorrow that cannot be expressed."

The day wore on; the child's condition became worse. Night fell, and it began to snow; the Indians made camp.

Mary was now so stiff from her own wound that she could neither sit nor stand. Her child was in the grip of a violent fever. "So it must be," she wrote, "that I must sit all this cold winter night upon the cold snowy ground, with my sick child in my arms, looking that every hour would be the last of its life; and having no Christian friend near me, either to comfort or help me."

The next day, the party moved on to the Indian village of Wenimesset. There, Mrs. Rowlandson nursed her little girl until she died one week later. "About two hours in the night," she then wrote, "my sweet babe like a lamb departed this life, on Feb. 18, 1676, it being six years and five months old. It was nine days from the first wounding, in this miserable condition, without any refreshing of one nature or another, except a little cold water."

Overwhelmed as she was by suffering and sorrow, Mary Rowlandson yet found the strength to go on living. She became the slave of Wetamoo, widow of Alexander, chief of the Pocassets. On February 21, the band was joined by Indians coming back from a raid on Medfield. One of these brought Mary the most precious gift that a Puritan woman in her predicament could wish. "I cannot but take notice," she wrote, "of the wonderful mercy of God to me in those afflictions, in sending me a Bible."

In Chapter 30 of the book of Deuteronomy, she read that the Lord promised mercy to sinners who repented, and that "though we were scattered from one end of the earth to the other, yet the Lord would gather us together, and turn all those curses [with which He had afflicted us] upon our enemies."

In the weeks that followed, Mary Rowlandson consulted her Bible many times. She drew from it consolation and the courage to go on living. One day, early in March, she felt dizzy: "My knees were feeble," she wrote, "my body raw...I cannot express the affliction that lay upon my spirit." Reaching for her Bible she began to read from the prophet Jeremiah: "Thus saith the Lord, refrain thy voice from weeping, and thine eyes from tears, for thy work shall be rewarded, and [the afflicted] come again away from the land of the enemy."

During the first few weeks following their assault on Lancaster, the Indians moved through the forests in a leisurely way, but at the beginning of March they began to quicken the pace when they found that the colonial militia was on their trail. Mary Rowlandson painted a vivid picture of the band hastening through the forest. "They marched on furiously," she wrote, "with their old and with their young. Some carried their old, decrepit mothers, some carried one and some carried another. Four of them carried a great Indian upon a bier; but going through a thick wood with him they were hindered and could make no haste. Whereupon they took him upon their backs and carried him, one at a time."

Coming to a river, the Indians improvised rafts to carry the people across. "They quickly fell to cutting dry trees," said Mrs. Rowlandson, "to make rafts to carry them over the river, and soon my turn came to go over. By the advantage of some brush which they had laid upon the raft to sit upon, I did not wet my foot, which cannot but be acknowledged as a favour of God to my weakened body, it being a very cold time." At this time she recalled a verse from Isaiah: "When thou passeth through the waters I will be with thee, and through the rivers they shall not overflow thee."

Mrs. Rowlandson noted, honestly enough, that God's providence seemed to protect the heathen Indian as much as herself in crossing the river, but that this protection did not extend to the white people who were pursuing them. "And here," she said, "I cannot but take notice of the strange providence of God in preserving the heathen. They were many hundreds, old and young, some sick and some lame, many had papooses on their backs, the greatest number at this time with us were squaws [women], and they travelled with all they had, bag and baggage, and yet they got over this river aforesaid."

The ease with which the Indians crossed the river was in marked contrast with the trouble that the colonial militia had. "On that very same day," she wrote, "the English army came after them to this river and saw the smoke of their wigwams, and yet this river put a stop to them. God did not give them courage to go over after us."

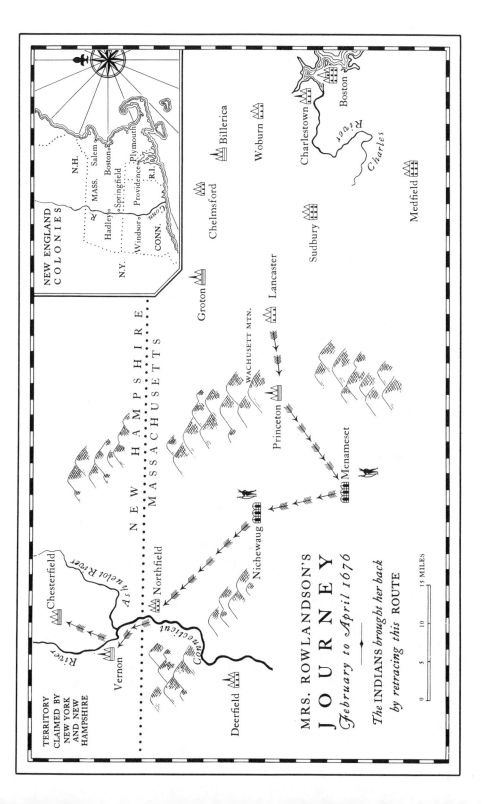

NEW ENGLAND
COLONIES

N.H.

MASS.   Salem

Boston

Springfield   Plymouth

Hadley   Providence   R.I.

Windsor   CONN.

N.Y.   CONN.

TERRITORY
CLAIMED BY
NEW YORK
AND NEW
HAMPSHIRE

N E W   H A M P S H I R E

M A S S A C H U S E T T S

Chesterfield

Assinelot River

Northfield

Vernon

River

Connecticut

Deerfield

Nichewaug

WACHUSETT MTN.

Princeton

Menameset

Lancaster

Groton

Chelmsford

Billerica

Woburn

Sudbury

Charlestown

Boston

Charles   River

Medfield

MRS. ROWLANDSON'S
J O U R N E Y
February to April 1676

The INDIANS brought her back
by retracing this ROUTE

0   5   10   15 MILES

Surely God, she thought, if the English had been ready to accept His favor, "would have found a way for the English to have passed this river, as well as for the Indians with their squaws and children and all their luggage."

In the days that followed, the Indians came to Northfield, on the Connecticut River, and took canoes to carry them across to join King Philip in South Vernon, Vermont. Coming ashore, Mary found herself amidst a large throng of Indian people who were on the riverbank. They were in a good mood, laughing and rejoicing over their victories. She burst into tears; this was the first time that she had wept in the presence of her captors. "Although I had met with so much affliction," she said, "and my heart was many times ready to break, yet could I not shed a tear in their sight, but rather had been all this while in a maze and like one astonished. But now I may say, 'By the rivers of Babylon I sat down and wept; yea, we wept when we remembered Zion.'"

Mrs. Rowlandson was taken to see King Philip, who invited her to sit with him and smoke; a courtesy which she refused. "This in no way suited me," she wrote, "for though I had formerly used tobacco, yet I had left it...It seems to me to be a bait, the Devil lays to make men lose their precious time...Surely there are many who may be better employed than to lie sucking a stinking pipe."

Mrs. Rowlandson refused King Philip's pipe, but hunger had long since taught her to eat Indian food that at the beginning she had found repulsive. At first, she wrote, "it was very hard to get down their filthy trash." Food that she felt she would rather have died than eat became, before very long, "sweet and savory to my taste." Among the items included in her new diet were parched corn, ground nuts or acorns, horsemeat and broth boiled from horses' bones.

Mrs. Rowlandson also made clothes for the Indians, and traded these for food. King Philip asked her to make a shirt for his son, for which he paid her a shilling with which she bought a piece of horseflesh. She also made a cap for the boy, in return for which Philip invited her to dinner. Dinner was a thick wheat pancake fried in bear's fat. "I thought," she wrote, "that I never tasted pleasanter meat in my life." She made another shirt for an Indian woman for which she received a piece of bear. "Another [woman] asked me to knit a pair of stockings, for which she gave me a quart of peas. I boiled my peas and bear together, and invited my master and mistress to dinner."

In the second week of March, Mary Rowlandson moved with the Indians back across the Connecticut River into New Hampshire. Early in April, they reached Chesterfield and began to retrace their steps, moving southwards into Massachusetts. The Indians were not now treating Mary unkindly; the malicious acts of a few, who threw ashes into her eyes or drove her from their wigwams out into the cold, were counterbalanced by the kindness of others who provided her with food and shelter. Her torments, now that she was used to the wilderness routine, were more mental than physical. Many times she would sit in a wigwam, dreaming of happy times in the past; and then "would suddenly leap up and run out, as if I had been at home, forgetting where I was and what my condition was." Quickly she came to her senses when she saw "nothing but wilderness and woods and a company of barbarous heathens."

For the last part of April and into May, the Indians were moving back into central Massachusetts. Negotiations for Mary's ransom were opened and were soon brought to a successful conclusion. She had the happiness of being reunited with her husband and her family.

The ordeal in the wilderness had provided Mary Rowlandson with a heightened insight into Indian life and its hardships. The colonists had calculated, she said, that if the Indians' corn supplies were destroyed they would be reduced to starvation and their resistance would come to an end. This was a serious miscalculation that did not take into account the passionate desire of Indian patriots to defend their land and their way of life, even if they had to die for their liberty. "I did not see," Rowlandson wrote, "all the time that I was among them, one man, woman, or child die with hunger. Though many times they would eat that which a hog or a dog would scarcely touch, yet by that God strengthened them to be a scourge to His people."

The staple articles of diet for the Indian people as they fled and fought in the wilderness were nuts, artichokes, roots, beans and weeds. "They would pick up old bones," Rowlandson wrote, "boil them and drink up the liquor, and then...eat them. They would eat horses' guts, and ears, and all sorts of wild birds which they could catch; also bear, venison, beaver, tortoise, frogs, squirrels, dogs, skunks, rattlesnakes; yea, the very bark off the trees." She marveled that God provided "for such a vast number of our enemies in the wilderness, where there was nothing to be seen, but from hand to mouth."

The struggle waged by King Philip and his people was in vain. Reduced to starvation in the winter of 1676, they were living, as Rowlandson had described, on roots and the bark of trees. Outnumbered by the New England soldiers nearly four to one, they were defeated and rounded up. The leaders were executed and the survivors made captive. Even though the colonists had need of labor to cultivate their lands, they did not use very many Indian slaves—it was too easy for them to flee to the woods and vanish forever. Most of the people who lost their freedom as a result of King Philip's War were shipped off to the West Indies and sold to planters there.

The tide of white settlement, which robbed the Indians of their lands and spelled the extinction of their way of life, moved inland in the central and southern colonies as well as in the northern ones. Settlers brought in European labor to help them clear the forests and to develop prosperous farms.

4

THE WOODS OF WILLIAM PENN AND HOW THEY WERE SETTLED

If thou buy a Hebrew servant, six years he shall serve: and in the seventh he shall go out free for nothing. If he came in by himself, he shall go out by himself; if he were married, then his wife shall go out with him.

Exodus

William Penn was an English aristocrat and a Quaker who, since his youth, had nourished the dream of founding a settlement in the New World where people might live freely and in equality—where they might be free to think and worship as they pleased and where, too, they might be free of the burdens of land tenure as these existed in the Old World. In 1680, he petitioned Charles II, king of England, to allot to him a tract of land in America, as settlement of a debt owed by the king to the Penn family.

Penn received his charter in 1681. Because the land and its control was vested in Penn and his heirs as sole proprietors, Pennsylvania was a *proprietary* colony. Other such colonies given by royal grant to individual proprietors were North and South Carolina, New York, New Jersey, and Georgia. Penn's charter gave him a princely estate—all the land in North America bound by 40° of latitude on the south to 43° on the north. The eastern boundary of the grant lay along the Delaware River.

This tract, with its woods and waters, its mines and its minerals, was to belong to Penn and his heirs forever as a freehold estate, paying to the king as his royal due two beaver skins yearly. "And of our further grace," said the king, "we have thought it fit to erect the aforesaid country into a province...and do call it Pennsylvania; and so from henceforth we will have it called."

Penn, as might be expected, was given the authority to govern his new estate. Since, the king said, he had special confidence in William Penn's wisdom and justice, he granted to him, his heirs or deputies, the power "to publish any laws whatever for the public uses of the said province by and with the advice and approbation of the freeholders or their delegates so they be not repugnant to the laws of this realm..." Penn, in other words, could rule Pennsylvania as he saw fit, but he was not an absolute ruler. Laws must be enacted with the consent of a provincial assembly representing the freeholders; no laws would be held valid by the king that were in conflict with British law and the rights that Britain's common law guaranteed to British subjects.

Both Charles II and William Penn were well aware that the province of Pennsylvania was very nearly the same size as England itself. It could not be developed without the labor of numerous immigrants. Penn, therefore, was authorized to recruit and transport settlers from Britain or other parts of Europe. "That this new colony," said the king, "may the more happily increase by the multitude of people resorting thither, therefore we...do hereby grant license to all the liege people present and future of us [that is, present and future British subjects] to transport themselves and their families into [Pennsylvania]..."

In the years that followed, Penn did a roaring business promoting immigration and the sale of his lands to prospective settlers. In 1683, he published a pamphlet in London describing the infant colony. Philadelphia had already been laid out; in a few years it would become a thriving port and America's leading city. It lay, Penn wrote, "between two navigable rivers, Delaware and Skulkill, thereby it hath two fronts upon the water, each a mile, and two from river to river." The location, he said, was ideal, and building had progressed rapidly. The town had grown within less than a year "to about four score houses and cottages, such as they are, where merchants and handicraftsmen are following their vocations as fast as they can, while the countrymen are close by on their farms."

Two years later, Penn estimated that there were about 7,000 people in Philadelphia and the settlements around it. The town then boasted more than 350 houses, some of them "large, well-built, with good cellars, three stories and some with balconies." City streets were named after the trees that grew in abundance in the surrounding forest— Mulberry, Chestnut, Walnut, Cranberry, Plum, Oak, Beech and many more.

Philadelphia was a port where people of many nations came to work and live, "French, Dutch, Germans, Swedes, Danes, Finns, Scots, Irish and English." Of these, the English were the most numerous. Penn then made the interesting observation that all these different people, living in the same place, bound by the same allegiance to the English king and to the laws of Pennsylvania, "live like people of one country." This "civil union," he said, was one of the reasons for Philadelphia's prosperity.

In 1685, Philadelphia with its surrounding farms was still a tiny community. A backbreaking job lay ahead, if the colony were to grow into a rich province, of clearing the forest, building houses, tilling the land and gathering the harvest. Manpower, not only in Pennsylvania but throughout the colonies, was a crying need if the settlers, both big landowners and small farmers, were to prosper and become wealthy.

Nobody realized this more clearly than Penn himself. "It is agreed on all hands," as he so precisely put it, "that the poor are the hands and feet of the rich. It is their labor that improves countries; and to encourage them is to promote the real benefit of the public." Penn noted that "there are abundance of these [poor] people in many parts of Europe, extremely desirous of going to America." Profit was to be made by both transporting these potential emigrants and putting them to work after they arrived.

Penn did not mention the Indians as a source of labor power. Nowhere in the colonial area was it possible for them to satisfy the whites' demands. Their numbers declined rapidly with the arrival of the Europeans as a result of enslavement, disease, war and flight. During the 17th century, the most popular solution to the labor problems— and this was particularly true in Pennsylvania and Virginia—lay in the importation of white workers from the British Isles and Europe.

Many people, as Penn said, were anxious to emigrate to America because of poverty, war or persecution, but they were unable to raise the necessary money for passage. So a bargain was struck between them and a number of middlemen—sea captains, merchants and landowners— who laid out the money required to bring them over. The emigrants in return bound themselves to labor for a specified number of years. They did this by signing contracts with those who provided the transportation. Such a contract, enforceable at law, was called an *indenture*; the emigrant who signed it was called an indentured servant, or, if under 21, an "apprentice."

The indenture specified the number of years for which the laborer must work in order to pay back the cost of transportation to the colonies. The owner of the contract in return provided transportation, and also food, clothing and shelter during the term of service. The employer was also bound to provide the worker, when he or she regained freedom, with certain equipment and land in accordance with "the custom of the country." A Massachusetts indenture of 1713 provided that:

Nicholas Bourguess, a youth of [the island of] Guernsey, of his own free and voluntary will, and by and with the consent of his present master, Captain John Hardy of Guernsey, aforesaid, mariner, has put himself as a servant unto Mr. William English, of Salem, in the county of Essex, within the province of Massachusetts Bay.

The term of labor for which Bourguess bound himself was four full and complete years; the youth undertook to labor well and faithfully at the command of his master. The bleakness of this life of endless toil without wine, the company of women or song, is captured in the dry words of the contract: "At unlawful games he shall not play; taverns and alehouses he shall not frequent; fornication he shall not commit, nor matrimony contract; but in all things shall demean himself as a faithful servant."

The master on his part undertook to provide "sufficient meat, drink, clothing, washing, and lodging, and, in case of sickness, with physic and attendance...and to learn him to read a chapter well in the Bible, if he may be capable of doing it." As for "freedom dues" the master agreed to provide "two suits of apparel for all parts of his body—the one for the Lord's day, the other for work days."

The trade in servants was a profitable one. The agents rounded up not only laborers and paupers, but also convicts, children and prisoners of war and shipped them to the New World. Some of these shippers, when the supply ran low, were not above kidnapping people and carrying them across the sea by force. The trade, in sum, was a terrible one. It inflicted great suffering during the transatlantic voyage, exposed workers in some cases to cruel treatment and brought about the separation of families. It has been estimated that as many as one-half of all the white people who immigrated to the American colonies south of New England came as contract laborers.

Early in the 18th century, a stream of immigrant labor began to flow to America from southwest Germany. Most of these people came to Philadelphia, and their story has been told by Gottlieb Mittelberger, who emigrated to Pennsylvania in 1750 and published his *Journey to Pennsylvania* in 1756. Mittelberger's purpose in writing was to expose the horrors of the sea voyage and to warn simple German peasants against the crafty emigrant agents and the Dutch sea captains who sought to lure unsuspecting people from their homes and sell them into bondage.

Germany's western boundary follows the valley of the Rhine. The river flows northward for more than 300 miles

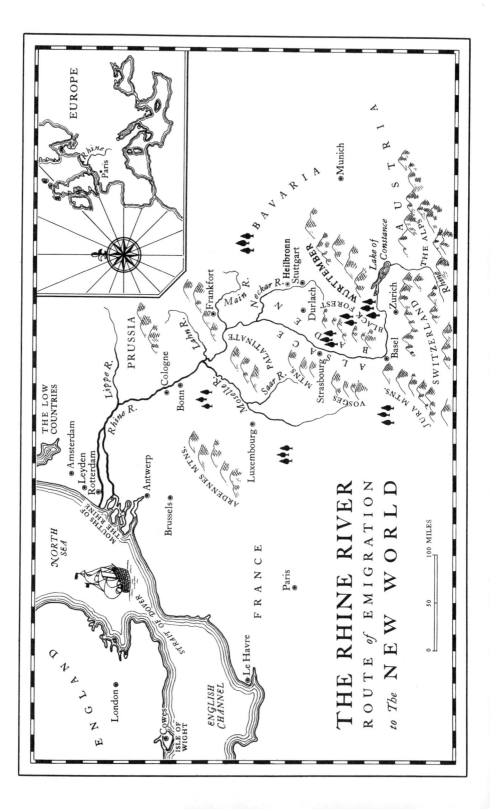

before turning sharply to the west, entering Holland and emptying its waters into the North Sea. Three German provinces, the Palatinate, Baden and Wurttemberg, border the Rhine in the upper part of its course.

In the 18th century, many small farmers inhabited this lovely country; their lives were made hideous by endless wars and the harsh oppression and avarice of their rulers. After 1700, agents were sent out from the Dutch ports of Rotterdam and Amsterdam that lie close to the mouth of the Rhine to promote among these people the idea of immigrating to America. Their purpose was to circulate literature promoting the idea of settlement in America. Traveling around the villages, these agents gave out literature, reading it out loud whenever they could gather a crowd. They described the New World in glowing terms. In America, they said, land was free and there was enough for all; in America there were no wars; a person could put white bread and meat on the table every day; there were few taxes, and what money was raised in this way was used to help the poor.

Debates broke out among the people. Father disputed with son, husband with wife. Some, finally, made the decision. Traveling chests were built and carefully packed; food was prepared for the voyage, for in those days sailing ships made little or no provision to feed emigrants. The family that did not have its own supplies for the long trip was in danger of starvation.

At length the great day arrived. The emigrants packed their chests on carts, made their way to Durlach or Heilbronn, and boarded a river boat for the long trip down the Rhine River to the sea. They had begun a journey, said Mittelberger, that would mean "for most who undertake it the loss of all they possess, of freedom and peace, and for some the loss of their very lives."

This process of ruin began long before the emigrants ever saw the sea. The Rhine boats, as Mittelberger pointed out, had to pass 36 separate customs houses between Heilbronn and their destination at the Holland ports. The endless delay, he said, "involves a great deal of expense for the passengers; and it also means that the trip down the Rhone alone takes from four to six weeks."

German emigrants in this 1805 drawing are shown at Basel on the boats that will take them the full length of the Rhine, from the Swiss border to the Netherlands ports 400 miles away. One boat is at the dock; the people are saying farewell to their families and friends . (Library of Congress)

When at last they arrived in Holland the emigrants had to transfer from the river boats to ocean-going vessels; another delay of five or six weeks took place. The people were obliged to start consuming the food and to spend the money that they had saved for the trip. Herded like animals onto the ships, they were packed into crowded quarters between decks. The more who made the trip, or so the shippers thought, the more would survive, and the greater the profits would be from their sale. "The people," wrote Mittelberger, "are packed into the big boats as closely as herring, so to speak. The bedstead of one person is hardly two feet across and six feet long, since many of the boats carry four to six hundred passengers."

The ships then crossed the English Channel and put in at the port of Cowes in order to take on more cargo. "Because of contrary winds," wrote Mittelberger, "it sometimes takes the boats from four to six weeks to make the trip from Holland to Cowes...On arrival everything is examined once more and customs duties paid. It can happen that the ships have to ride at anchor there from eight to fourteen days, or until they have taken on full cargoes."

This final delay completed the ruin of many emigrant passengers. They had planned to pay their own way to the British colonies, but now their money was gone and their supplies wasting away. Everybody, as Mittelberger pointed out, "has [had] to spend his last remaining money and to consume the provisions that he meant to save for the ocean voyage." Even before the ordeal of the transatlantic trip had begun, many self-respecting farmers found themselves reduced to total destitution.

At last the ships weighed anchor and headed westward down the English Channel and out into the wide Atlantic. The voyage to Philadelphia would take 7 to 12 weeks to complete. "During the journey," said Mittelberger, "the ship is full of pitiful signs of distress—smells, fumes, horrors, vomiting, sea sickness, fever, dysentery,...scurvy, cancer, mouth-rot and similar afflictions, all of them caused by the age and the highly salted state of the food,...as well as the very bad and filthy water, which brings about the miserable destruction and death of many." There were other afflictions too. "There are so many lice, especially on the sick people," wrote Mittelberger, "that they have to be scraped off their bodies."

Misery reached its climax when there was a storm. "The sea," wrote Mittelberger, "begins to surge and rage so that the waves often seem to rise up like high mountains, sometimes sweeping over the ship." The ship heaved and tossed. "Nobody aboard can either walk, sit, or lie down; the tightly packed people on their cots…are thrown every which way."

The emigrants were overcome with panic and despair. They began to quarrel bitterly. "Often," said Mittelberger, "the children cry out against their parents, husbands against wives, and wives against husbands, brothers against sisters, friends and acquaintances against one another."

Many were overcome with the pain of homesickness, groaning "Oh! If only I were back home, even lying in my pigsty!" Others, feeling the torments of hunger and thirst, would exclaim "Ah, dear God, if I only had once again a piece of good bread or a fresh drop of water." Some, overwhelmed with the thought "that many hundreds of people must necessarily perish, die, and be thrown into the ocean," fell into a deep depression from which it was impossible to arouse them. "In a word," concluded Mittelberger, "groaning and lamentation go on day and night, so that even the hearts of the most hardened, hearing all this, begin to bleed."

The sufferings that the voyage imposed did not fall on all with the same intensity. Women and children endured more than men. "One can scarcely conceive what happens at sea," wrote Mittelberger, "to women in childbirth and to their innocent offspring. Very few escape with their lives." As for little children between the ages of one and seven, he said, they "seldom survive the sea voyage; parents must often watch their offspring suffer miserably, die, and be thrown into the ocean." The parents grieved all the more because their little ones were swallowed up by the ocean; there would be no graves to visit, to deck with flowers and to mourn by.

In Mittelberger's opinion, unsanitary and crowded conditions below decks were the principal causes of the high mortality that prevailed. Next, he singled out tainted food and water as a major cause of death. "It is not surprising," he wrote, "that many passengers fall ill, because...warm food is served only three times a week, very bad, very small in quantity, and so dirty as to be hardly palatable. The water distributed in these ships is often very black, thick with dirt, and full of worms. Even when very thirsty one is unable to drink it without loathing."

After many weeks of sailing, the travelers finally caught a glimpse of land. People already half dead revived and crawled up from below decks to gaze at America from afar. "They cry for joy," said Mittelberger, "pray, and sing praises and thanks to God."

For the vast majority, there was little cause for rejoicing. Only immigrants who had money to pay for their passage, or who could provide good security, were allowed to leave the ship. The others remained on board as prisoners. Their modest savings had been used up buying necessities of life between the time that they left their homes in Germany and the moment, many weeks later, when their ship actually left England and embarked on the transatlantic voyage. They owed the sea captain a debt because he had transported an entire family without being paid. This debt could be "redeemed," or paid off, only if the captain sold these people to American farmers for a term of years. These "redemptioners" would be obliged to labor hard without pay for several years before winning their freedom.

As the immigrants waited aboard the ship, this traffic in human beings began. The arrival of a ship from Europe bringing freight and servants was news in the port of Philadelphia. The announcement was printed in the newspapers; the word was passed along rapidly in town and the surrounding countryside. Would-be purchasers flocked to the ship from miles around. "Every day," wrote Mittelberger, "Englishmen, Dutchmen, and Germans come from Philadelphia and other places, some of them very far away...and go on board the newly arrived vessel that has brought people from Europe and offers them for sale." These buyers looked over the human cargo and selected the strongest and the healthiest. Then they drove the hardest bargain they could. "When an agreement has been reached," said Mittelberger, "adult persons by written contract bind themselves to serve for three, four, five or six years, according to their health and age."

In order to leave the ship, many parents were obliged to sell their children as well as themselves. Greedy speculators might buy whole families, split them up and then sell them again. This led to inhuman suffering. "It frequently happens," Mittelberger observed, "that parents and children do not see each other for years on end, or even for the rest of their lives."

No matter what an immigrant's age, life in the New World proved to be one of hard, endless toil. "Work," as Mittelberger said, "is strenuous in this land, and many who come into the country at an advanced age must labor hard for their bread until they die." He listed a number of the backbreaking jobs that young and old people were forced to do: felling oak trees, cutting the timber, leveling great tracts of forest, roots and all. "Our Europeans who have been purchased," he noted bitterly, "learn from experience that oak tree stumps are just as hard in America as they are in Germany."

Once cleared, the forest lands were laid out in fields and meadows; this was done in typically American pioneer style. "People," wrote Mittelberger, "construct railings or fences around the new fields...All meadows, all lawns, gardens and orchards, and all arable lands are surrounded and enclosed by thickly cut wood planks set in zig-zag fashion one above the other. And thus cattle, horses and sheep are confined to pasture land."

German immigrants to Pennsylvania may be thought of as temporary slaves, bound to perform for a term of years whatever tasks their masters set them to. Goaded by hard toil and hard treatment, these servants might take flight. In fleeing, they broke the law, which was written especially to safeguard a master's right to the labor that he had purchased. In later years, these laws, developed in order to recapture white fugitive servants, were used with equal effect to retrieve black fugitive slaves. "No one," as Mittelberger said, "can run away from a master who has treated him harshly, and get very far. For there are regulations and laws that ensure that runaways are certainly and quickly recaptured. Those who arrest a fugitive get a good reward. For every day that someone who runs away is absent from his master he must as a punishment do service an extra week, for every week an extra month, and for every month a half year."

Yes, a servant's life was hard. A wife or a husband may have died on the ocean and the children scattered no one knew where. Those who landed on America's shores could at least thank God for delivering them from the terrors of the sea; uncounted ships bearing emigrants from Europe suffered shipwreck and sank into the ocean or were battered to pieces on the shores. But still the immigrants came. Every year thousands more Germans, carried on dozens of ships, landed in Philadelphia.

Their term of service over, many Pennsylvania servants took their freedom dues and moved inland to carve out farms for themselves. Scotch, Irish and German pioneers moved west and southwest to clear and settle the interior valleys and uplands of Pennsylvania, Virginia and North Carolina.

In the Southern colonies, just as in Pennsylvania, the poor proved to be "the hands and feet of the rich." There was one important difference. White labor by itself proved insufficient to meet the needs of Southern planters, who turned to the importation of black workers as well.

5

OUTPOST OF EMPIRE: Virginia and Its Planters in the 17th Century

I brought you into a plentiful country, to eat the fruit thereof; but when ye entered, ye defiled my land, and made mine heritage an abomination.

The Words of Jeremiah

In December 1606, a group of adventurers left London on the *Phoenix* to cross the Atlantic and to settle in Virginia. John Smith, a young English sea captain and soldier of fortune, was a member of this group. Six years later, he published a *Description of Virginia*. "Here," he wrote, "are mountains, hills, plains, valleys, rivers and brooks all running most pleasantly into a fair bay [surrounded] with fruitful and delightsome land."

Virginia, with its bright sun, serene sky and refreshing rains, was carpeted with wild flowers. "Almost all the year long," as Robert Beverley wrote in 1705 in his *History and Present State of Virginia*, "the levels and vails are beautified with flowers of one kind or another, which makes their woods as fragrant as a garden."

Here in Virginia, Britain launched its first serious effort at the colonization of North America. A fort and settlement were established in 1607 at Jamestown on the James

River. Two years later, the London Company, a group of nobles and merchants who had financed this venture, secured a charter from the king, James I. This charter was not unlike that which established the Massachusetts Bay Company 20 years later, but the London Company, unlike the Massachusetts venture, was set up with a view to immediate profit. The promoters hoped to secure quick returns from their investment in the form of precious metals like gold and silver. Since the operation proved more expensive than they had anticipated, they invited the public, in 1609, to invest their money and become partners in the undertaking.

The campaign to sell shares and secure funds was launched by the publication of a pamphlet that bore the quaint title *Nova Britannia, offering most excellent fruits by planting in Virginia.*

Nova Britannia, or New Britain, is an interesting example of a new type of promotional literature that for many years was directed at Europeans, urging them to invest in the New World or immigrate to it. The pamphlet explained why an overseas empire was likely to be a profit-making enterprise for British investors and merchants. This idea about overseas empire, written up and further expanded, came to be known as *mercantilism*. Mercantilism explains much about Britain's attitude toward its American colonies. It also helps us to understand why, more than 150 years after the founding of Jamestown, the rulers of Britain would prefer war rather than grant the colonists their independence.

Nova Britannia's author, who remains unknown, began with a statement of his purpose in writing the pamphlet: to persuade the English to support the colonization of Virginia either by providing money for the venture or by immigrating there themselves. This work, he said, would advance the glory of God by bringing the light of Christian faith to the Indians, "millions of men and women, savage and blind, that never yet saw the true light shine before their eyes, to enlighten their minds and comfort their souls." It would honor the king, Charles I, and would provide support for "that small number of our friends and countrymen already planted [that is, settled] in Virginia.

John Smith was one of the first 17th-century colonizers of Virginia who left an important account of his experience there and later explored the New England coast. This engraving was made in 1616, when Smith was 37 years old. A drawing based on the engraving appeared on the explorer's Map of New England, *published in London that same year.*
(Library of Congress)

Also, the venture would be "for the singular good and benefit" of all those who chose to invest in the project or to join the immigrants who planned to settle in the new colony.

Nova Britannia's author conceded that the effort to settle Virginia had a long and discouraging history, going back to Sir Walter Raleigh's ill-fated explorations of 1584–87, but he brushed this aside. The London Company was now on a sound business footing with a new charter issued in 1609; its purpose was to develop Virginia and bring the profits of exploitation back to England. People could lend their money to the Company with confidence that the investment would be a sound one.

Virginia, it was pointed out, was a rich land whose produce when sold on the European markets would bring a bountiful return. The country was full of minerals and different kinds of wood "of which we have a lack in England." The soil was very fertile, or "strong and lusty of its own nature." It would yield precious commodities such as silk, skins and furs, lumber, sturgeon and caviar, dyes and many other costly things of which "we know not yet, because our days are young."

As for the ships that would transport the cargoes to and from England, they would move swiftly and safely across the Atlantic. "The voyage," wrote *Nova Britannia*'s author, "is not long or tedious…Our course and passage is through the great ocean where is no fear of rocks or flats, nor subject to the restraint of foreign princes. Most winds that blow are apt for us, and none can hinder us." Virginia's harbors, too, he said, were excellent. "When we come to the coast there is continual depth enough, with good bottom for anchor to hold."

The author then turned to the Indian peoples who inhabited Virginia, and whom he described as "a wild and savage people that live and roam up and down in troops like herds of deer in a forest." What right, might it be asked, did the English have to invade a foreign land and drive out its peaceful inhabitants? The Indians, he answered, were "loving and gentle," eager to welcome the English and to learn the ways of a more advanced civilization. The Indians would come to understand that the

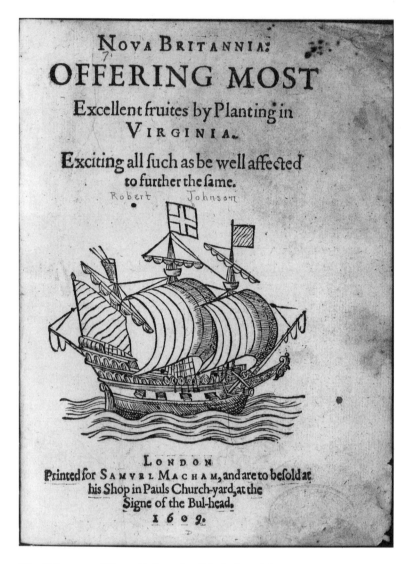

The title page of Nova Britannia. *It is to be sold, we are informed, at Samuel Macham's "Shop in Paul's Church-yard." St. Paul's was one of the oldest and most famous of London City churches. The Church-yard was a center where the sale of books thrived.* (Library of Congress)

English wished to settle in Virginia without driving the earlier inhabitants away. The hope was "to bring them from their base condition to a far better: first in regard to God the Creator, and of Jesus Christ their Redeemer, if they will believe in him; and secondly, in respect of earthly blessings,..."

Among the "earthly blessings" that the Indians might expect to receive as a result of their contact with the English would be clothes. In Virginia, the writer pointed out, "there is want of sheep to make woolen cloth, and this want of cloth must always be supplied from England." As the colony grew, the demand for cloth would grow. English merchants would prosper both by the sale of American goods on the European market and by the sale of manufactured materials, especially cloth, in America. In this way Virginia might become the first outpost of a new commercial empire. England, "this little northern corner of the world," would be "in a short time the richest storehouse for merchandise in all Europe."

But these dreams would not be realized, the writer pointed out, unless immediate steps were taken to supply the pressing needs of the Jamestown venture, both in terms of people and of money. He considered that the first of these, the supply of labor to clear the land and bring it under cultivation, was no problem. Enough workers could be found if only the funds were forthcoming to enable them to be shipped over and put to work. "Our land," he said, "abounds with swarms of idle persons, who hav[e] no means of labor to relieve their misery." These "swarms" could be shipped off to Virginia and put to useful work.

The company also needed, in addition to rough labor, "painful" men, that is, honest craftsmen who worked hard or "took pains" at a skilled trade. Many such skills were needed in building a colony:

"Be they never so poor, so they be honest, and painful, the place shall make them rich: all kinds of artificers we must first employ, as carpenters, shipwrights, masons, sawyers, bricklayers, ploughmen, sowers, planters, fishermen, coopers, smiths, metalmen, tailors, turners, and such like, to make and fit all necessaries for comfort and use of the colony."

In 1612, the company's charter was modified. The company was given permission "to take, lead, carry, and transport" to Virginia any people of British or foreign origin who would "willingly accompany them in the said voyages...; with shipping, armor, victuals, and all manner of merchandises and wares, and all manner of clothing, implements, furniture, beasts, cattle, horses, mares, and all other things necessary for the said plantation."

But the early settlement of Virginia did not go, by any means, as easily as the author of *Nova Britannia* had predicted. In 1624, the king canceled the 1612 charter of the London Company after a long period of strife and inner turmoil in its administration. Virginia thus became the first *royal* colony in British America. It was brought directly under the rule and supervision of the king and his agents. This was by contrast to the situation in corporate colonies such as Massachusetts or proprietary colonies such as Pennsylvania, where the administrative authority remained in the hands of private companies or individuals. In a royal colony, the governor was appointed by the crown and was directly responsible for his actions to the king in London. The new situation thus brought about in Virginia was clearly stated in Charles I's Royal Proclamation of 1625. Said the king:

Our full resolution is that the government of the colony of Virginia shall immediately depend upon ourself, and not be committed to any company or corporation to whom it may be proper to trust matters of trade or commerce, but cannot be safe or fit to communicate the ordering of state affairs...that at our own charge we will maintain those public officers and ministers, and that strength of men, munition, and fortification, as shall be fit and necessary for the defence of that plantation.

The royal governor of Virginia, as in the other colonies, had to rule with the help of a popularly elected assembly. The first such assembly met at the insistence of the colonists in 1619; until 1670, all freemen—that is, men who were neither servants nor slaves—had the right to vote for representatives to that body.

After 1624, tobacco soon became Virginia's staple crop. It grew so well on the fertile soil and there was such demand for it in Europe that raising tobacco for export seemed to be the easiest and most profitable way for the average farmer to make a living. The London Company, which had founded the colony, was now a thing of the past; but London merchants began to make money by sending their ships to Virginia to pick up the tobacco and bring it home for sale on the English and continental markets. This meant that Virginia planters specialized so completely in raising this one crop that many of the manufactured goods they needed had to be imported from England—exactly as *Nova Britannia* had predicted. "They have their clothing of all sorts from England," wrote Robert Beverley in 1705, "as linen, woollen, silk, hats and leather...though their country be overrun with wood, yet they have all their wooden ware from England; their cabinets, chairs, tables, stools, chests, boxes, cartwheels, and all other things, even so much as their bowls, and birchen brooms, to the eternal reproach of their laziness."

Englishmen began to flock to Virginia to take up the land and make their fortunes from tobacco. But these early comers faced the same kind of problem that presented itself to the ambitious planter in Pennsylvania: To become rich in the New World, a man must not only have land, but also *hands and feet*—the labor of many poor "painful" people to cut down trees, to root out stumps, to build houses, to split rails, to plough, to sow and to harvest.

The planters turned first to white indentured servants in order to solve this problem of labor scarcity. As the author of *Nova Britannia* had pointed out, there was no lack in England of poor and unemployed farm workers; to add to the supply, prisoners were taken from the jails or people were seized on the streets and whisked off to ships bound for Virginia; Irish and Scots prisoners, captured in England's wars, were transported to the shores of the New World. All were sold by the shippers into servitude.

These indentured servants did the backbreaking work of clearing the forest and cultivating the land. At the same time, by their labor and their very *presence*, they helped create the tobacco aristocracy, the group of wealthy planters that by the end of the century had emerged as the effective rulers of this region. By a Virginia law specially designed to stimulate the importation of servants, any person who introduced settlers into the colony was entitled to receive 50 acres of land for each servant thus brought in. This was known as the headright system. It speedily became the basis for fraud and abuse. The merchants who shipped servants, the planters to whom these people were sold, even the seamen who manned the ships on which the servants came, could, and did, swear that they had imported servants into the colony. All demanded to be rewarded with 50 acres of land per person imported.

From this it was but one step to bribing the registrars to enter on the colony's books land titles for as many acres as a man might want. Thus, a group of owners emerged who owned title to thousands of acres of Virginia's choicest land. This tobacco aristocracy was a tiny group, but it exercised a power over the colony and its destiny that was out of all proportion to its actual numbers.

At the other end of the social scale, many poor servants, as soon as their appointed term of service was over, took up little farms on the frontier and in the back woods. The colony became divided into planters and their servants on the one hand, freemen and ex-indentured servants on the other. In 1650, the population of Virginia was only 15,000; by the end of the century, it had grown to 70,000, the vast majority of whom were poor white farmers living on small farms in a land of large properties and big estates.

During the 17th century, few black slaves were brought to Virginia. As late as 1670, there were perhaps not even 2,000 of them, as compared with 6,000 white indentured servants; but by 1720, these figures were reversed. The number of slaves continued to grow throughout the 18th century. What happened in Virginia also happened with more or less speed in other Southern colonies—in Maryland, in South Carolina and in Georgia.

How are we to explain the fact that a society, the majority of whose members were originally free white farmers, turned into one dominated by rich planters and the labor of black slaves?

After 1660—the year that Charles II was restored to the throne in England—the mass of Virginia's ordinary tobacco farmers became rapidly estranged from the "establishment," from the imperial system and the men who controlled it in London and in Jamestown. Low prices for tobacco meant low income and widespread distress; the situation was made worse by a series of new taxes that the assembly imposed in 1674 for a variety of purposes. The burden of these taxes fell heavily on the common people. Agents had to be sent to England to contest with the king the transfer of a large tract of northern Virginia to the ownership of royal favorites; to cover this expense, the assembly "laid a tax of fifty pounds of tobacco per head, for two years together, over and above all other taxes, which was an excessive burden." In order to finance the cost of justice, taxes were laid on every case that was tried, "which taxes," wrote Robert Beverley, "fell heaviest upon the poor people, the effect of whose labor would not clothe their wives and children."

The unsettled state of the frontier added to these woes. A succession of Indian raids took a number of lives and spread panic among the frontier people. Thomas Matthew, who was a well-to-do farmer in Northumberland County, wrote that settlers fortified their houses against attack with palisades and redoubts. Men went into the fields with arms in their hands; some stood guard while others worked. "What was remarkable," said Matthew, "I rarely heard of any houses burnt, though many were abandoned, nor ever of any corn or tobacco cut up or other injury done." The settlers' panic, nonetheless, was not without reason. Here and there small groups of whites had been ambushed and assassinated. Frontier people, too, remembered wholesale massacres of which whites had been the victims in 1622 and again in 1640.

The frightened settlers selected Colonel Nathaniel Bacon as their leader. Bacon, the son of an English gentleman, had arrived in Virginia only two years earlier, in 1674, and had then acquired extensive lands on the frontier. Bacon was a fine orator and a natural leader. "He was young, bold, of inviting appearance and powerful elocution," as one observer put it. The frontier people flocked around him. Bacon promised his followers that he would not lay down his arms until he had taken revenge on the Indians and had won redress for other grievances of which the settlers bitterly complained.

Bacon decided to ask the governor, Sir William Berkeley, for permission to launch a military campaign against the Indians. His request for a commission—for authorization, that is, to make war on Indians—at once produced a collision between Bacon and the governor. Sir William had ruled Virginia for many years and had enjoyed much popularity with its people. Refusing Bacon's request, Berkeley immediately became a target of popular hatred. Hundreds of Bacon's men descended on Jamestown, determined to obtain by force what Berkeley would not grant of his own free will.

Dramatic scenes followed. At the end of July 1676, Berkeley fled eastward across Chesapeake Bay to Accomack County. As Robert Beverley tells it, Berkeley, "who had been almost the idol of the people, was, by reason of the loyal part he acted, abandoned by all, except some few who went over to him from the western shore in sloops and boats."

On July 30, Bacon issued a *Declaration of the People* from the Middle Plantation, six miles from Jamestown. He denounced Berkeley for levying unjust taxes and for failing to provide the people with proper defense against the Indians. Charging that Berkeley had sent for troops from England to suppress the uprising, Bacon administered an oath to his followers, "that we, the inhabitants of Virginia, do oppose and suppress all such forces of that nature."

At this point, Berkeley seized the initiative. Gathering together a tiny force of loyalist men and ships, he attacked Jamestown and reoccupied it on September 8. Thus began an armed struggle between Bacon's army of small farmers, frontier planters, indentured servants and a few Negro slaves, against Governor Berkeley and the crown itself.

On September 19, 1676, the rebels in their turn seized Jamestown and burned it to the ground. Virginia's capital was described as a settlement with "twelve new brick houses besides a considerable number of frame houses with brick chimneys." But the rebellion received its death blow when Bacon died of fever the following month. The rank and file of his army abandoned the cause scattered and fled back to their homes. By the end of 1676, Berkeley had seized and executed the ringleaders and was in full control of the situation.

Thus ended an historic revolt. Virginia tidewater planters emerged from the struggle stronger and more affluent than they had been before and in a good position to take advantage of a booming European tobacco market and rising tobacco prices. By 1706, no less than 300 ships were engaged every year in bringing English goods to Virginia's wharves and returning home laden with the Virginia leaf.

The failure of the smaller Virginia farmers and backwoods people to win their struggle against the governor and crown marked a turning point in Southern history. By the time of Bacon's rebellion, the established planters of the Virginia tidewater were beginning to tap a fresh source of cheap labor with which to plant and harvest their crops: slave labor from Africa. This, as it seemed to them, was to be preferred to the labor of rebellious white servants who, after working for a few years, flocked off to the frontier to hack out homes of their own. Black slaves could be had in indefinite numbers and they could be compelled to work not just for a few years, but for life. Purchased on the African coast and brought to America against their will, they were to provide a new foundation for planter rule and merchant wealth.

6

THE BLACK FOUNDATION: Bringing Africans to the New World

Thus saith the Lord God: "Behold, I lay in Zion for a foundation stone, a tried stone, a precious corner stone, a sure foundation.

The Vision of Isaiah

The importation of white servants was more or less adequate for the needs of New England and the central colonies—New York, New Jersey and Pennsylvania. But the Southern colonies, first of all Virginia and South Carolina and later Georgia, developed a need for labor that indentured servitude, temporary and limited as it was, could not satisfy. In these Southern colonies, the climate and the natural fertility of the land made possible and profitable large-scale agricultural operations—the production of crops not principally for the use or consumption in the colonies themselves but for export to the English and European markets. These crops were tobacco in Virginia and North Carolina, indigo and rice in South Carolina and Georgia.

The cultivation of these crops under the hot summer sun was grueling work. A man conceivably might undertake the production of crops for his own advantage, but who, unless he were forced, would want to kill himself toiling on another man's land, to harvest another man's crop, to live and die so that some big Virginia or South Carolina landowner might grow rich? Thus, white labor proved increasingly hard to come by in the South. For an indentured servant, flight to the frontier was a relatively easy matter; and, in any event, the indentured servant was bound by law only to *temporary* servitude. The big planters, therefore, who, by the end of the 17th century, had won control of the rich river valleys along the Southern coastal plain, were obliged to look around for another source of labor. They found what they sought in the importation of slaves from Africa.

At the mouth of the Gambia River, at 13° north latitude, the coast of Africa begins a mighty sweep toward the east, continuing eastward for close to 2,000 miles before it once more turns south beyond the delta of the Niger River. This is the coast of Equatorial Africa that became known to Europeans in the 15th century through the explorations of Prince Henry of Portugal and his sailors and navigators. It was a low-lying, steamy, tropical, palm-fringed and fever-ridden area which white men called the Coast of Guinea.

When they first began to survey the African coast, the Portuguese seafarers captured a few Africans and brought them back to Europe as something of a curiosity. The main reason that the Portuguese had in rounding the Gulf of Guinea was to find gold and "elephants' teeth," not to look for slaves.

But in the 16th century, the objectives of the African trade changed. Spain was developing her empire in Central America and Hispaniola (Haiti and the Dominican Republic of today). The demand of the Spanish settlers for labor to work their mines and sugar plantations became infinite; they began to seize slaves on the Guinea Coast and ship them to the American plantations.

At first, permission of the Spanish crown—the *assiento*—to ship slaves to the colonies was given only to

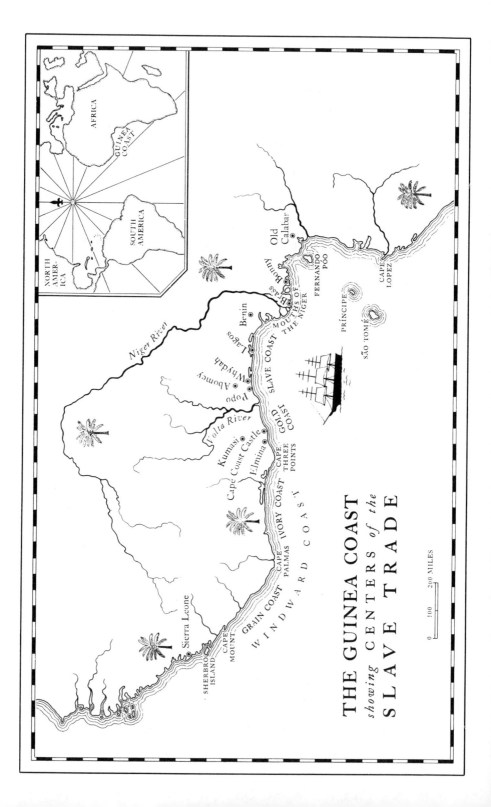

THE GUINEA COAST
showing CENTERS *of the*
SLAVE TRADE

Spaniards. But soon merchants from other countries, greedy for profit, began to raid the Guinea Coast and carry off Africans to the New World. It was only a step to winning the *assiento* and developing a trade that would supply not just Spanish settlements in the New World but French and British ones as well.

In 1672, Charles II of England issued a charter to a group of Englishmen, authorizing them to organize the slave trade under the title of the Royal Africa Company. Under this grant of power, the Royal Africa Company was given the sole right to establish settlements on the west coast of Africa and to carry slaves in English ships—the British slave trade, in other words, was to be a monopoly in the hands of the "adventurers" empowered to carry it on. The Royal Africa Company was authorized to have its own official seal: "on the one side the image of our Royal Person in our Parliament or royal robes, on the other side an elephant bearing a castle supported by two Negroes or blackamoores."

The Royal Africa Company could not maintain its monopoly very long in the face of French and Dutch competition; and it had only limited success in suppressing British and American "interlopers"—merchants and seamen, that is, who were not members of the company but who sailed to the Guinea Coast, took slaves and sold them in America for their own profit.

The slave trade reached its height in the 18th century. The British alone possessed a fleet of slavers that numbered more than a thousand vessels and transported between 5,000 and 15,000 slaves a year from Africa to the New World. European and American shippers made profits from this business whose total can hardly be estimated. Alcohol, iron, firearms, tobacco, cloth, blankets, pewterware, carpets and rugs were shipped to the Guinea Coast and traded for slaves. The slaves were then shipped to the Caribbean islands and to the American mainland, where they were exchanged for sugar, tobacco and gold.

Along the Guinea Coast, African chiefs kept the slave market well supplied with an endless stream of fresh victims. This was done in various ways, but especially by war. John Barbot, an employee of the French trading companies, made several voyages to the Guinea Coast between 1678 and 1682; he wrote an account of his experiences that tells much. "The trade in slaves," he said, "is in a most peculiar manner the business of kings, rich men, and merchants." These people, having received their victims from the actual slave hunters, then sold them to white traders at the coast. The slaves, wrote Barbot, were "for the most part prisoners of war, taken either in fight, or pursuit, or in the incursions they make into their enemies' territories."

The Gold Coast, lying to the west of the Volta River, furnished most of the slaves. It was the central portion of the Guinea Coast and the main theater of operations for both British and Dutch. At Accra on the Gold Coast, the enslavement of neighboring peoples by acts of war was a never-ending business. "This country," wrote Barbot, "is continually at war with some of the neighboring nations, which are very populous and from whom they take very many prisoners, most of whom they sell to the Europeans."

Some of these captured people had to be brought from distant inland places for sale at the seashore. Many arrived after the long journey, said Barbot, in very poor condition "by reason of the barbarous usage they have had in traveling so far, being continually beaten and almost famished." Not only adults, but children too were stolen and sold. Many of these children, said Barbot, were seized in the cornfields "at the time of the year when their parents keep them there all day to scare away the devouring small birds, that come to feed upon the millet in swarms."

In times of famine, people were driven to sell themselves into slavery in order to escape death from starvation. "When I first arrived at Senegal in December 1681," wrote Barbot, "I could have bought a great number at very easy rates, if I could have found provisions to subsist them, so great was the dearth in that part of Nigritia."

Along the coast whole communities might earn their living from the slave trade. Barbot described Great Bandy in the delta region of the Niger River. It was a township with about 300 houses that stood in marshy ground. The people of this and other such settlements did a thriving

African men and women, tied together in a coffle
and with their hands bound behind their backs,
trudge under guard toward the coast. (Library of
Congress)

business with inland chieftains, trading fish for ivory and slaves. "By means of long and large canoes," wrote Barbot, "some sixty foot long and seven broad, rowed by sixteen, eighteen, or twenty paddlers [they] carry European goods and fish to the upland blacks; and bring down to their respective towns, in exchange, a vast number of slaves, of all sexes and ages, and some large elephants' teeth, to supply the Europeans trading in the [Niger] river."

Thus through wars, raids, kidnapping and barter, the slaves came into the possession of the coastal chiefs. These chiefs made their fortunes trading their fellow countrypeople to the whites in exchange for pots and pans, trinkets and beads, carpets, kettles and guns. Barbot, hoping perhaps to make the white man's crime seem less, carefully described the cruelty of the African chieftains and slave traders. "The slaves" he wrote, "are barbarously treated by their masters who feed them poorly and beat them inhumanly, as may be seen by the scabs and wounds on the bodies of many of them when sold to us. They scarce allow them the least rag to cover their nakedness...When dead, they never bury them, but cast the bodies out into some by-place, to be devoured by birds, or beasts of prey."

When the slaves arrived at the coast, they were placed in compounds near the beach. The chiefs then summoned the white traders to come and examine their stock. When the Europeans were ready to receive them, all the slaves were marched "out into a large plain, where the surgeons examine every part of every one of them, to the smallest member, men and women being all stark naked." In this process the Europeans accomplished *triage*; that is, they separated the young and healthy slaves of both sexes from the old, the infirm, the sick and the diseased. The defective people having been set on one side, the rest were branded like animals. "Each," said Barbot, "is marked on the breast with a red-hot iron, imprinting the mark of the French, English, or Dutch companies, so that each nation may distinguish their own."

The branded slaves were then returned to the compounds to await embarkation on the slavers bound for America and the Caribbean. At some places, they were housed in "factories" that the Europeans' companies had built. These factories were trading posts stockaded for protection against outside attack, and sometimes they possessed facilities for the storage of slaves. Many days and nights might pass before the Africans were loaded on the ships and taken into exile. The seas often ran high on the slave coast; black breakers crested white broke angrily on the shore and made it impossible for the long canoes to be launched.

The time of embarkation now drew near when the slaves were loaded onto the canoes to be taken out to deep water where the slavers rode at anchor. It was a time that captains and their crews dreaded; many Africans preferred resistance and death to the fate that the whites had in store for them. "The Negroes," wrote Captain Phillips of the slave ship *Hannibal*, "are so loth [unwilling] to leave their own country, that they have often leaped out of the canoes...into the sea, and kept under water till they were drowned, to avoid being taken up and saved by our boats, which pursued them."

Captains of slaving vessels received a fee for each voyage that depended directly on the number of slaves whom they stowed as cargo below the main deck. Thus greedy commanders had a powerful inducement to cram as many Africans as they could into their ships. This cruel overcrowding resulted in a high death rate among the captives. Agents of the Royal Africa Company reported to London that high losses of healthy slaves at sea were due to no other reason than "the covetousness of commanders."

Loading completed, the ships put out to sea. The slaves were fed a simple diet of corn flour mixed with water and boiled into a kind of porridge; this was supplemented several times a week with beans. Many Africans, overcome with despair, wished only to die and they went on hunger strikes. In spite of every effort made to force-feed them, Captain Phillips said, "they will starve to death..."

On some ships, the slaves were brought up on deck once a day and made to take exercise. Captain Phillips noted that "...it was my hard fortune to have great sickness and mortality among the slaves...," even though he used to bring them up on deck and "...make them jump and dance for an hour or two to our bagpipes, harp, and fiddle, by which exercise to preserve them in health." Mortality was, indeed, high on most slave ships, though here the Dutch had a better record than others. A loss of 12% to 15% of the slave cargo dying at sea was not considered out of the ordinary. The journal kept by Captain Peter Blake, of the Royal Africa Company, on a voyage from the Gold Coast to the West Indies on the *James* during the years 1675–76, records the deaths at sea. The following entries are typical:

[One woman] being very fond of her child, carrying her up and down, wore her to nothing, by which means she fell into a fever, and died.

[One man] died of a fever, by lying in the long boat in the rain in the night, which no man knew of, for he went there privately.

Some of the captives preferred revolt to the stench and the slow death of the crowded slave quarters between decks. John Casseneuve, first mate of the *Don Carlos* of London, described such a revolt that took place in 1701. "The slaves," he said, "had eaten their midday meal on deck, and were about to go down below after being served each his pint of water. Armed with knives, pieces of iron, and broken shackles, they suddenly assaulted the crew." The crew opened fire on the slaves, killing some and wounding many. The survivors retreated and took cover. "Many of the most mutinous," said Casseneuve, "leaped overboard and drowned themselves in the ocean with much resolution, showing no manner of concern for life." Nearly 30 slaves lost their lives before this rebellion was subdued.

In the 17th century, most slaves imported to the New World from Africa were sent directly to the Caribbean or the West Indies. As time passed, an increasing number were imported directly to the mainland colonies—to all of them, not just the Southern ones. In New England, the original Puritan ban on the use or sale of slaves was gradually set aside. Early in the 18th century advertisements such as the following were becoming commonplace in the *Boston News Letter*:

Three Negro men and two women to be sold and seen at the house of Mr. Josiah Franklin at the sign of the Blue Ball in Union Street, Boston.

August 13, 1713

To be sold, a parcel of Negroes, just arrived,...men, women, boys and girls; they are to be sold at Capt. Nathaniel Jarvis' house near Scarlett's wharf.

September 1, 1726

Just imported from the coast of Guinea, and to be sold on board the Schooner Post-boy, Robert Ball master, lying at Mr. James Russell's wharf in Charleston [Massachusetts], a parcel of likely young Negro boys and girls. Inquire either of said Ball on board said schooner, or of said Russell at his warehouse on said wharf.

August 23, 1744

In Rhode Island, New England's second most important trading center, the story was the same. A law of 1652 forbade the importation of slaves, but it was quietly ignored. After 1708, slaves were imported from the West Indies, and Rhode Islanders were commissioning ships to be built in New England ports especially for the African trade. News of this trade appeared in the newspapers. The *Boston News Letter*, for example, reported on June 8, 1738, a disaster that befell Captain Godfrey Malbone of Rhode Island. Malbone's "very fine sloop" "was totally consumed by the lightning on the coast of Guinea, with a great many Negroes on board. Capt. Caleb Godfrey, commander, and his company saved their lives by taking to the long boat." The "company" that the paper referred to was Godfrey's crew. For Malbone, the owner, the loss was a great one because not only his vessel was destroyed but his valuable slave merchandise as well.

By 1750, the slave trade was booming, and Rhode Islanders enjoyed their own substantial share of it. They made their profits primarily by selling slaves in the West Indies in return for gold and molasses. The molasses was brought back to New England and converted into rum; taken to Africa, this was turned once more into slaves, and these again on the return trip were converted into molasses and gold.

Rhode Islanders played little part in supplying the slaves that were imported from the Guinea Coast and then sold in the mainland colonies—primarily to the tobacco and rice growers of the South. A Swiss visitor to Virginia, Franz Michel, reported in 1702 that most of Virginia's wealth was in slaves, "for if one has many workmen, much foodstuff and tobacco can be produced." Virginia's slaves, he said, were brought in every year in large numbers on English ships. "They can be selected," he said, "according to pleasure, young and old, men and women. They are entirely naked when they arrive, having only corals of different colors around their necks and arms."

Virginia's African-American population increased from about 6,000 in 1700 to 30,000 in 1730. In South Carolina, the rise in the slave population was even more dramatic. In 1715, there were no more than 10,000 slaves in the colony; by 1730 the number had risen to 40,000. In the years that followed, about 1,000 Africans were brought in every year to toil on the Carolina rice and indigo plantations.

Most American slaves were field slaves, condemned to a lifetime of hard labor without compensation, for the benefit of others. Slaves were exposed to every type of cruelty and abuse; white men rightly feared their anger and their revenge. Wherever there were slaves, numerous laws were passed to discourage their flight and to punish rebellion.

Flights, plots and acts of revenge were frequent in many colonies, the laws against them notwithstanding. In New York City, for example, five slaves were hanged and one was burned at the stake in 1741 merely because they had been *accused* of having set fire to a building. No evidence was offered at their trial to prove that they were guilty as charged. These executions prompted a Bostonian to write that "the cruelty and inhumanity the Negroes have met with is...rife in the English plantations." The colonists, said the writer, must "stop making bonfires of the Negroes and perhaps loading ourselves with greater guilt than theirs. For we have too much reason to fear that the divine vengeance does and will pursue us for our ill-treatment to the bodies and souls of our poor slaves."

Seven years before the trial and execution of these six New York slaves, the city had been the scene of a famous event: the trial of John Peter Zenger.

7

MARTYR IN MANHATTAN: Governor Cosby and the Trial of Peter Zenger

> *Freedom of speech is a principal pillar in a free government: when this support is taken away, the constitution is dissolved, and tyranny is erected on its ruins. Republics and limited monarchies derive their strength and vigor from a popular examination into the actions of the magistrates.*
>
> *James Alexander*

On Tuesday last his Excellency William Cosby, Esq., Governor of this province, arrived at Sandy Hook in his Majesty's ship Seaford, Captain Long, commander, in seven weeks from Great Britain, and landed here about 10 o'clock, in the evening, and was received at the water-side by several gentlemen, who attended him to the fort. The next day between the hours of 11 and 12 his Excellency walked to the City Hall, where his commission was published.

In these words the *Boston News Letter* announced the arrival in New York City, on August 1, 1732, of William Cosby, the new governor. The scene was a gay one, as the people thronged the broad, tree-lined streets to catch a glimpse of their new ruler as he rode by amid a company of pikemen and a troop of horse.

Fort George was William Cosby's residence until his death a few years later, in 1736. The fort lay at the very tip of Manhattan Island. The city streets, laid out in spacious and regular avenues, clustered around it. The dwelling houses were set amid gardens with peach trees in bloom. High gables and neat whitewashed interiors testified to the Dutch origins of the settlement. Some of the houses had balconies on the roofs with wooden fences to keep children from falling. Here the inhabitants might sit in the cool of the evening enjoying the view—across the river to the green hills of Brooklyn or northward up Manhattan with its quiet meadows, orchards and farms.

New York had been settled during the 17th century, at the same time as Virginia and for much the same reasons. Both colonies were organized as commercial ventures, from which it was hoped that a profit might be taken by the "adventurers." In the case of Virginia, it was the London Company; in the case of New York, the Dutch West India Company. Trading posts were established at the tip of Manhattan Island and at Albany; efforts were set afoot to attract settlers and to develop "plantations." The organizers and owners of such settlements were known as "patroons": They were granted extensive privileges and rights in terms of landownership, trading concessions and government in return for bringing over settlers from Europe.

New Amsterdam, as New York City was first called, did not prosper under the Dutch. The gradual spread of the white settlement provoked the anger of the Indians just as it had done in New England and Virginia. In 1643, a party of the Dutch massacred more than 100 Indians, and this bloody act touched off a struggle that lasted for two years. The Dutch West India Company found its New York colony a drain on its resources that it was unable to bear, and in 1664 the British crown took possession without a struggle. A royal charter was issued, conferring New York on James, duke of York, the brother of Charles II, king of England. James, as an individual, became the proprietor,

*This drawing, looking westward across the East
River, shows New Amsterdam at the middle of the
17th century. The fort is at the left, with a windmill
beyond. Houses of the settlement are clustered
loosely around.* (Library of Congress)

or owner, of New York. James also received the usual rights of landownership, commerce and government.

Even after the British takeover, New York was not settled as rapidly as Pennsylvania. Unlike William Penn, James did not throw his colony open to settlement by small farmers or dissenters. Vast tracts of land were given away to influential people. The export of grain and lumber from these big estates, along with the fur trade, remained for many years the most important element in the New York economy.

The duke of York ruled his colony through governors whom he himself appointed. He didn't worry about such things as representative assemblies or popular elections. For many years, the people of Staten Island, Long Island and Westchester, where there were numerous small farms, were denied a voice in the government. In response to pressure from freeholders such as these, the governor of the province in 1682 issued "writs of election," and a representative assembly finally came into being. The assembly at once enacted a Charter of Liberties listing the rights of British citizens. The basic right thus declared was the right of all freeholders to vote for the election of representatives to the assembly "without any manner of restraint or compulsion."

James vetoed the Charter of Liberties when he became king of England in 1685. Turbulent times followed. In 1688, James was driven from his throne by revolution in England. In New York, Jacob Leisler, soldier and merchant, overthrew the royal governor, assumed control of the province and called a representative assembly into session. Leisler was put down, but his movement was an important one. It established a tradition of united action by the poorer settlers, both British and Dutch, against the rule of the provincial aristocrats.

In the years that followed, quiet returned to New York and trade flourished. By 1730, the city's population had grown to more than 7,500; New York, next to Boston and Philadelphia, had become the biggest town in the country. The New York Assembly was now composed of two houses: the upper house, or governor's council, and the lower house numbering about 30 members chosen by the freeholders in public elections.

The New York Assembly met as soon as William Cosby arrived in 1732 and voted him an annual salary of £1,500. Cosby was not impressed; he was, as a matter of fact, angry that the assembly had not voted him more. Cosby was a soldier, a member of the aristocracy and a professional servant of the crown. This was his first trip to the New World; New York meant little to him beyond a new job and a new opportunity for self-enrichment.

Cosby soon antagonized New York citizens. The first of them was Rip Van Dam, a wealthy merchant and a member of the governor's council. Rip Van Dam had served as deputy governor during the full year that had passed between the death of the previous governor, John Montgomerie, in July 1731, and Cosby's arrival in August 1732. Cosby claimed one half of Van Dam's salary for himself, and this Van Dam refused. An unseemly squabble followed when the governor decided to take Van Dam to court and sue him for this money. Soon the colony was in a ferment. People had long memories of autocratic rule and favoritism in New York. If a rich, powerful man like Van Dam could be disgracefully treated, what, they asked themselves, would the future hold in store for humbler people? The colony became divided into two parties: a small but influential group of aristocrats and officials for Cosby and an opposition headed by eminent lawyers, landowners and merchants enjoying a measure of popular support.

Rip Van Dam and the opposition needed a newspaper to voice their views. They selected John Peter Zenger as their printer. Zenger was an immigrant from the Palatinate; in 1710 when he was 13 years old, he had come to New York City with his family. John Peter's father had died on shipboard; his mother apprenticed the lad to the New York City printer William Bradford. The apprenticeship lasted eight years until the young man was 21. Later he married Anna Catharina Maulin, a young teacher, and settled down to earn a scanty living operating a print shop.

In November 1733, Zenger issued the first number of *The New-York Weekly Journal, containing the freshest Advices, foreign and domestic.* James Alexander, a leading New York lawyer and member of the opposition, was the

Journal's mastermind. The *Journal*, as Alexander wrote to a friend, was "designed to be continued weekly and chiefly to expose Cosby and those ridiculous flatteries with which [editor] Harrison loads our other newspaper."

The "other newspaper" which Alexander referred to was the Cosby administration's organ, *The New-York Weekly Gazette*. The *Gazette*'s printer was none other than William Bradford, with whom Zenger had served his long apprenticeship.

The articles appearing in Zenger's *Journal* were unsigned and written by the leaders of the opposition. Eagerly awaited and widely read, the articles delivered biting attacks on Cosby and his friends. As James De Lancey put it, the writers "with the utmost virulency have endeavoured to asperse [blacken] his Excellency and vilify his administration." De Lancey, hardly 30 years old, was a New York supreme court chief justice and a strong Cosby supporter.

In September 1734, elections were scheduled for New York City; magistrates and council members were to be chosen in each ward. As election day drew near, Cosby summoned a number of leading citizens, including city officials, to the Fort and invited them to sign an address praising his administration. But this address did not sway the voters; they expressed their disapproval of Cosby and his administration by electing all of the opposition candidates, save one. It was a stinging defeat for the governor.

Amid general rejoicing, a number of victory ballads were composed, printed and hawked about the streets. One song praised the voters for their courage in standing up to be counted:

> *To you good lads that dare oppose*
> *All lawless power and might,*
> *You are the theme that we have chose*
> *And to your praise we write:*
> *You dared to show your faces brave*
> *In spite of every abject knave;*
> *with a fa la la.*

Cosby and his party were furious at this setback. Unable to find out who his critics were, the governor issued two proclamations on November 6, 1734, urging citizens to "discover"—that is, publicly identify and accuse—those who had written the election songs and the anti-administration articles that had been appearing for the year past in the *The New-York Journal*. But no citizen came forward to finger the people who had written the songs or *Journal* articles.

The administration then issued a warrant and had Zenger arrested on November 17 "for printing and publishing several seditious libels dispersed throughout his journals or newspapers." The reason given for arresting the printer was that the publication of the *Journal* was a breach of the King's peace, "tending," as the warrant put it, "to raise factions and tumults among the people of this province, inflaming their minds with contempt of his Majesty's government."

Zenger was lodged in the city jail and denied the right to communicate with anybody. The publication of the *Journal* was disrupted, but, after some delay, an issue finally appeared. Zenger apologized to his readers for the inconvenience and offered an explanation. "I was put under such restraint," he explained, "that I had not the liberty of pen, ink, or paper, or to see, or speak with people."

Zenger's lawyers complained about his plight to the supreme court, he informed his readers, and the situation improved a little. He was now permitted to speak through the prison door to Anna Catharina and his apprentices and give them instructions. "So I doubt not," he concluded, "you'll think me sufficiently excused for not sending my last week's *Journal*; and I hope for the liberty of speaking through the hole of the door of the prison, to entertain you with my weekly *Journal* as formerly. And am your obliged humble servant, John Peter Zenger."

James Alexander was one of Zenger's lawyers. He asked the court to grant bail so that his client might go free until trial. Judge De Lancey set bail at £400, but Zenger was a poor man and the sum was far beyond his means. He remained in jail for eight months until his trial in the summer of 1735.

Zenger's supporters, as far as is known, made no attempt to raise the sum that De Lancey demanded. Zenger was deprived of his liberty even though he had merely been *accused* of a crime and had not yet had his day in court, much less been convicted on any charge. This was an act of tyranny. New York's Charter of Liberties, as well as the Bill of Rights enacted by Parliament in 1689, decreed that *excessive bail ought not to be required*. Defiance of this rule violated Zenger's right to go free until the day of his trial. It was, too, a warning to New Yorkers: there would be more acts of tyranny if they failed to oppose this one.

All the time that John Peter Zenger remained in jail, the *Journal* continued to be printed and circulated under Anna Catharina's direction. The trial opened on August 4, 1735, at New York's City Hall, located at the intersection of Wall Street and Nassau Street. On the bench were the two chief justices, James De Lancey and Frederick Philipse. Richard Bradley, the attorney general, read the governor's complaint, or "information," to the 12-man jury, but first he introduced himself. He was, he informed the court, "the Attorney General of Our Sovereign Lord the King, for the Province of New York, who for our said Lord the King in this Part prosecutes." He came to court, said Bradley, "in his own proper person" to accuse Zenger of having committed the crime of seditious libel. He wished the court "to understand, and be informed, that John Peter Zenger,...did cause to be printed and published, a certain false, malicious, seditious libel, entitled *The New-York Weekly Journal*."

Bradley proceeded to explain to the jury what the law meant by the term "seditious libel." A libel, he said, was a written attack on a person's reputation. To libel a person in this way was a grave offense since it endangered the public peace. This, he went on, is clear when you consider that a person's reputation is his most precious possession. Libelous attacks enrage the victim and may cause him to commit violence in revenge.

But, Bradley continued, libels were even more serious when they were directed at public figures like magistrates, judges, or members of His Majesty's administration. Such attacks were called *seditious* libels because they not merely threatened the public peace but could also lead to sedition, or revolt. "What greater scandal can there be," asked Bradley, "than to have corrupt or wicked magistrates to be appointed by the King, to govern his subjects under him?" Bradley proceeded to quote and to comment upon selected passages from *The New-York Journal*, showing how disloyal they were.

The judges, James De Lancey and Frederick Philipse, listened with approval. Bradley had made an able exposition of the law of libel as it had been shaped by the courts and common law of England; he had shown that *The New-York Journal* was a libelous publication. All that remained for the attorney general to do was to prove to the jury's satisfaction that, as a simple matter of fact, Zenger had published and printed *The New-York Journal* and caused it to be circulated. The jury would then have no alternative but to deliver the verdict: "guilty of publishing, printing, and circulating *The New-York Journal* as charged." The court would then proceed to sentence Zenger to a stiff fine and a term in jail. This would mark the end of seditious writings in the royal province of New York.

A successful outcome to the trial, from the viewpoint of Cosby and his party, was all the more certain, because Zenger's lawyers, James Alexander and William Smith, no longer represented him. De Lancey had taken the precaution, several months earlier, of declaring on a flimsy pretext that both men were guilty of contempt of court. He ordered that they "be excluded from any farther Practice in this Court, and that their names be struck out of the Roll of attorneys." Thus when Zenger came up for trial, he faced formidable accusations with only a young inexperienced court-appointed lawyer to help him.

At this moment an old man, white haired and bent, rose in court. The attorney general and the justices watched with consternation. This was Andrew Hamilton, attorney general for the province of Pennsylvania. Hamilton was known as the most eminent lawyer in all of British America. At James Alexander's urgent invitation, he had come all the way from Philadelphia in order to defend John Peter Zenger.

Hamilton's argument was based on a brief that James Alexander had specially prepared; it had a certain simplicity. Zenger, Hamilton admitted, had indeed published the writings that were mentioned in the prosecution's "information" and that the prosecution charged were 'false.' He then posed this question: What if Zenger's statements were true—would they still be seditious? His answer was, no: "The falsehood," he said, "makes the scandal, and both make the libel...[T]o save the Court's time and Mr. Attorney's trouble, I will agree, that if he can prove the facts charged upon us to be false, I'll own them to be scandalous, seditious, and a libel."

This was too much for the chief justice, who told Hamilton that "you cannot be admitted to give the truth of a libel in evidence. A libel is not to be justified; for it is nevertheless a libel that it is true." De Lancey was here stating the old English legal principle "the greater the truth the greater the libel." It was a principle that had long been used in the English courts to suppress *any* statements that the government didn't like—and in particular attacks on evil practices that happened in fact to be only too true. Hamilton's argument, that people must have freedom of speech and press in order that they may tell the truth, was breathtaking in its boldness. A thrill ran through the courtroom as he denounced the old English doctrine as "monstrous and ridiculous."

Hamilton made clear that in saying this he was not talking at all about libeling of private individuals: "If the faults, mistakes, nay even the vices of a person be private and personal, and don't affect the peace of the public, or the liberty or property of our neighbour, it is unmanly and unmannerly to expose them either by word or writing." But with people in public life the situation was entirely different. "When a ruler," he said, "brings his personal failings but much more his vices into his administration...this will alter the case mightily." Free men, he insisted, "have a right publicly to protest the abuses of power,...to put their neighbours upon their guard against the craft or open violence of men in authority, and to assert...their resolution at all hazards to preserve [liberty], as one of the greatest blessings that heaven can bestow."

Hamilton was explaining that the abuse of power by those in authority was one of the supreme dangers that free men must always guard against if they valued their freedom. "Power," he said, "may justly be compared to a great River which, while kept within due bounds, is both beautiful and useful; but when it overflows its banks...it bears down all before it, and brings destruction and desolation wherever it comes." Liberty, he said, and the struggle to keep it, is the only defense that mankind has against "lawless power, which in all ages has sacrificed to its wild lust and boundless ambition, the blood of the best men that ever lived."

Old as he was, said the speaker—he was in his seventies—he was ready to use the rest of his life in the service of liberty. He was ready to go to the most distant part of the land if he could help quench "the flame of prosecutions upon informations" set on foot by the government to deprive the people of their right to resist the tyranny of men in power. "The question before you, gentlemen of the jury," he concluded, "is not of small or minor concern, it is not the cause of a poor printer, nor of New York alone, which you are now trying. No! it may in its consequence affect every free man that lives under a British government on the mainland of America. It is the best cause. It is the cause of liberty." Render a just and impartial verdict, he urged the jury; thereby you will help to win for us and our children a natural and legal right: "the right of exposing and opposing arbitrary power by speaking and writing truth."

The jury withdrew and soon returned with a verdict of "not guilty." At once, Zenger reported, "there were three huzzas in the hall, which was crowded with people, and the next day I was discharged from my imprisonment." Andrew Hamilton was borne away by his delighted supporters for a dinner at the Black Horse nearby to celebrate the victory. When he departed for Philadelphia, cheering crowds accompanied him through the streets while ships' guns boomed in the harbor. Two years later, John Peter Zenger was appointed official printer to the city. He died in 1746 at the age of 49.

The Zenger case is a milestone in the history of the struggle for a free press and in the growth of the idea of freedom itself. In this respect, it has contributed a key element to the legacy of freedom that comes to modern Americans from colonial times. The right of the people to speak the truth about their government and to know the truth about its deeds is a pillar of our democratic tradition and of democratic rule.

In 1734–35, during the time of Zenger's arrest, imprisonment and trial, events were occurring in the Connecticut Valley that were to have an important impact on the practice of religion in America and the right of the people to freedom of worship.

8

THE FOUR WINDS
Jonathan Edwards and the
Great Awakening

*The sun shall be darkened and the moon shall not give
her light, and the stars shall fall from heaven...and
they shall see the Son of Man coming in the clouds of
heaven with power and great glory. And he shall send
his angels with a great sound of a trumpet, and they
shall gather together his elect from the four winds.*

Matthew

It was a fine October morning in the fall of 1740. Nathan
Cole, a Connecticut farmer, was working in his fields when
a man ran up and told him that George Whitefield, a
famous English revivalist, would preach at 10 o'clock in
the parish of Middletown, 12 miles away. Cole at once
rushed off to saddle his horse. He and his wife mounted
up and trotted away as fast as they could go.

As the Coles went along, they saw a great cloud ahead
of them. At first Cole thought that it came from the
Connecticut River, but then he realized that it was dust
raised by the pounding of horses' hooves. "I could see," he
wrote, "men and horses slipping along in the cloud like
shadows." People on horseback were streaming down the
road toward Middletown, "scarcely a horse more than his

length behind another, all of a lather with foam and sweat, their breath rolling out of their nostrils."

When the Coles reached the Middletown meetinghouse, they found it surrounded by a huge crowd of people. Men and women thronged into Middletown and some were being ferried across the Connecticut River from the eastern side. The country all around lay empty. "I saw no man at work in his field," said Cole, "but all seemed to be gone."

George Whitefield stepped forward onto a platform that had been set up in front of the meetinghouse. He was a young man, only 25 years old, but already a legendary figure. Since first landing in Georgia in 1738, Whitefield had traveled the length and breadth of America preaching the Gospel and calling souls to repentance. "When I saw Mr. Whitefield come upon the scaffold," remembered Cole, "he looked almost angelical; a young, slim, slender youth before some thousands of people with a bold undaunted countenance."

When Whitefield began to preach, his message stabbed his listeners like a knife. As Cole put it, "he gave me a heart wound." This message was delivered not only by Whitefield but many other pastors during the 1730s and 1740s. It set America ablaze.

The first settlers in the 17th century were people of Protestant belief fleeing from persecution and hard times in the Old World. Although Catholics came to Maryland and Jewish immigrants to New York and Rhode Island, the majority of colonists everywhere in British America continued to be of Protestant background and convictions.

Protestant religious services in the New World were notable, for the most part, for their unadorned simplicity. The meetinghouses or churches were simple one-room wooden structures, often with bell tower and spire, whitewashed inside and out, furnished with bare wooden benches and pews and perhaps a potbellied stove to take the edge off the winter chill. Windows were of clear glass; there was no stained glass, statuary or ornamentation, except the candle sconces or candelabra. Few musical instruments found their way into the meetinghouses, at least at first—nothing except the unadorned voices of the worshippers singing psalms in unison. During the 18th

century, stringed instruments and choral singing gradually made their appearance in some places as part of the
ritual of the service.

Most Protestant congregations had an ordained minister whose function it was to deliver the sermon and to
conduct the service. In most Protestant churches, again,
there was a pulpit occupying a central place in the meetinghouse. The pulpit was the desk on which the Bible
rested; the Bible, in turn, was the foundation of Protestant
religion. It was the revealed word of God, the authority on
which the moral and political law of the community was
based. It was the minister's function, as a person who had
been specially trained for that purpose, to explain the
Bible to the congregation and help them to understand its
message. The minister's sermon, therefore, had an important part to play in most Protestant churches. In some
cases, it ran to great length—as much as two or even three
hours.

As time passed, the religious inspiration that had fired
the early colonists began to wane. The number of people
living in many of the older settlements increased. A never-
ending stream of immigrants moved westward to carve out
homes in the back-country. British America was growing
so fast that its churches could not keep pace with the
situation. More and more Christian people found themselves living outside the bounds or beyond the reach of any
organized church or congregation.

This situation presented both a personal and a community crisis. Life in colonial America was hard and dangerous, medical skill was both primitive and scarce, and death
was no stranger in the life of the average family. Many
babies died at birth; many mothers died in childbirth.
Fever and disease took a high toll. Death lurked everywhere in the form of snakes' fangs, falling trees, flooded
rivers, icy nights and Indian raids. What if man, woman
or child was not prepared for death? The colonists came
from a Christian tradition that taught that sinful human
beings could do nothing, achieve nothing, on their own—
salvation was beyond the realm of possibility for an unrepentant, unchurched sinner. Damnation and everlasting
torment awaited the souls of those who had no thought for

God, who did not strive for penitence and who made no struggle to follow a Christian path.

The settlers needed the church to prepare them not only for death, but also for life as part of the larger community of believers. As time passed, many, trapped in an isolated, hand-to-mouth existence, became aware of a great personal loneliness that spelled alienation not only from God but from each other. In those days, there was no community outside of the church; the only community was a community of believers who lived a common life and shared a common hope of salvation.

Traditionally, the church had enjoyed a monopoly of education. Its function was to instruct the people, and especially the children, in the meaning of the Christian life, Christian conduct and Christian law. Protestant children in particular must know the Bible, and they could not do that if they did not know their letters. People without a church, therefore, were people not only without moral leadership but without educational provision for their children.

This situation led to the religious movement known as the Great Awakening. The most impressive of several such movements that took place during the colonial era, was so named because it "awakened" thousands of people to the reality of Christian experience and the need for religion as a rule by which to live and as a key to the meaning of life itself. From Georgia to Maine, traveling ministers known as "itinerants" took their message to the people wherever they could gather a crowd—in the streets and on the town commons, in meetinghouses, in the open fields and even in the forests.

These itinerants were skilled in speaking directly to an audience, reaching its mind and touching its heart. Poor sinners that you are, they said, if God calls you to Him, to face the final judgment, how will it be with you? Have you repented of your sins? If not, how will you hope to escape His just anger? Jonathan Edwards, for example, one of the greatest of itinerants, struck terror and remorse into the hearts of his listeners with words such as these from a famous sermon delivered at Enfield, Connecticut in 1741:

This old meetinghouse at Hingham, Massachusetts was built in 1681 and is still standing. (Library of Congress)

*O sinner! consider the fearful danger you are in: it is a
great furnace of wrath, a wide and bottomless pit, full of
the fire of wrath, that you are held over in the hand of that
God, whose wrath is provoked and incensed as much
against you, as against many of the damned in hell: you
hang by a slender thread, with the flames of divine wrath
flashing about it, and ready every moment to singe it, and
burn it asunder; and you have no interest in any Mediator
[i.e., Jesus Christ], and nothing to lay hold of to save
yourself, nothing to keep off the flames of wrath, nothing
of your own, nothing that you have ever done, nothing that
you can do, to induce God to spare you one moment.*

After the explosion of fear, anger, sorrow and joy that
such words evoked, many people were prepared to become
"as brands plucked from the burning." New congregations
were formed, meetinghouses built, schools established. As
a result, the American people became bound together more
closely by their faith, the heritage that it transmitted from
the past, the vision that it held of the future.

The Great Awakening was made possible by years of
patient work undertaken by pastors like Jonathan Edwards who strove to educate their own congregations and
to train new ministers to carry their message to a wider
public.

Jonathan Edwards was the son of Timothy Edwards,
pastor of East Windsor, Connecticut. Timothy Edwards
settled in East Windsor in 1694 when it was a frontier
community with no meetinghouse and no organized congregation. There his son was born in 1703. Reverend
Edwards, like everybody else in the neighborhood, was a
farmer; Jonathan no doubt did his share of the family
chores. The majesty of America entered into his soul. "I
walked alone," he wrote, "in a solitary place in my father's
pasture. And as I was walking there, there came into my
mind a sweet sense of the majesty and grace of God that I
know not how to express." An ecstatic sense of the presence
of God amid the shining rivers, green fields and towering
trees of his native land runs through his earlier writings.

At the age of 13, Jonathan entered Yale College. In those
days, when there were no secondary schools, young people

entered college at a much earlier age than they do today. Yale was, in 1716, only 15 years old. Like all colonial colleges it was set up primarily to train "diligent young men of Christian piety" for service to the people as ministers. Edwards studied philosophy and theology; it seems that he was a priggish youth who disapproved of the amusements that his fellow students enjoyed. In a letter to his father, he complained about their "stealing hens, geese, turkeys...unseasonable nightwalking, breaking people's windows, playing at cards, cursing, swearing."

Edwards graduated from Yale in 1721. In 1727, he was called to Northampton, Massachusetts to assist his grandfather, the Reverend Solomon Stoddard. Northampton lay only a few miles upriver from East Windsor; it was a thriving frontier town, largest of many settlements in the broad and beautiful Connecticut Valley. When Stoddard died in 1729, Edwards succeeded to his ministry. He began to deliver simple but powerful sermons that hammered on the plight of sinners—the need that they had for repentance and Christ's saving grace if they were to escape eternal damnation.

Under Edwards' leadership, the first stirrings of the awakening began to make themselves felt in the Connecticut Valley. Edwards himself described in detail what happened in his *Faithful Narrative of the Surprising Works of God*. This was a long letter—one might call it a prose masterpiece—in which Edwards related the events that began to unfold in Northampton and the surrounding countryside during the early 1730s.

During his first two years in Northampton, Edwards wrote, there was no general awakening; it was, as he put it, "a time of dullness in religion." The young people in particular seemed to care little about eternal life and were absorbed in their own private pleasures: drinking in the tavern, partying, staying up all night to dance and make love. "Indeed," Edwards sadly remarked, "family government did much fail in the town."

Worst of all, when they attended Sunday meeting the young people made no secret of their indifference to the church. They were, as Edwards termed it, "indecent in their carriage"—making eyes at each other and carrying on whispered conversations. Edwards did not blame the young people too much for this disorder. The situation, he observed, "doubtless would not have prevailed to such a degree, had it not been that my grandfather, through his great age...was not so able to observe them."

Gradually, after Edwards became pastor, the mood of the community began to change. In 1734, a young man died suddenly at the village of Pascommuck, three miles from Northampton. Soon after, a young woman became very ill. As she lay dying, she urged people to seek the grace of Jesus and to give thought to the salvation of their eternal souls. "She died," said Edwards, "full of comfort in a most earnest and moving manner, warning and counselling others."

These two deaths triggered the New England awakening. An "earnest concern," wrote Edwards, "about the great things of religion, and the eternal world, became universal in all parts of town, and among persons of all degrees, and all ages...The only thing in their view was to get to the kingdom of heaven." People began to meet together in private houses to talk about the state of their souls, and to pray. "Such meetings," said Edwards, "were very greatly thronged." At Sunday meeting, "the congregation was alive in God's service, everyone earnestly intent on the public worship, every hearer eager to drink in the words of the minister, as they came from his mouth; the assembly in general were, from time to time, in tears while the word was preached; some weeping with sorrow and distress, others with joy and love, others with pity and concern for the souls of their neighbors."

The new inspiration of the congregation found its expression in the singing of the psalms. This had been an important part of Puritan worship from the very beginning. So much importance did the first settlers in New England attach to this that they had made their own translations from the original Hebrew. The *Bay Psalm Book*, which made these translations available to the New England congregations, was published at Cambridge, Massachusetts in 1640. It was the first book ever to issue from a press in British America. At Northampton, under Edwards, these psalms were sung in four parts, the men

*This carving is from a 1716 tombstone in Stratford,
Connecticut.* (Library of Congress)

carrying three and the women one, an indication that the congregation must have given much time and attention to the musical aspects of the service.

The awakening, starting in Northampton, soon spread up and down the Connecticut Valley to South Hadley, Suffield, Deerfield, Hatfield, Springfield and Long Meadow. "Many that came to town," said Edwards, "on one occasion or another, had their consciences smitten, and awakened, and went home with wounded hearts...till at length the same work evidently began to appear and prevail in several other towns in [Hampshire] county." The Massachusetts awakening began to link up with awakenings that had developed in Connecticut—at Windsor, Coventry, Stratford and other centers.

The New England awakening was part of a wider movement that had begun to develop independently in other parts of the country. Reverend William Tennent was preeminent among the leaders in the central colonies. He founded his Log College at Neshaminy, Pennsylvania in 1735 to prepare young men for the ministry and to spread the message of the awakening. The Log College was soon renamed the College of New Jersey, and, when it finally settled at Princeton, Princeton University. As for the South, the flames of the awakening were kindled there when George Whitefield came to Georgia in 1738. His arrival marked the first of a series of tours in which he preached to congregations throughout the country.

The awakening possessed an appeal that transcended age, gender or social status. What Edwards noted with respect to Northampton was true everywhere. The movement, he said, "has been extraordinary on account of the universality of it, affecting all sorts, sober and vicious, high and low, rich and poor, wise and unwise." He added one significant observation. "There are," he said, "several Negroes, that from what was seen in them then, and what is discernible in them since, appear to have been truly born again in the late remarkable season." At the time of the awakening, African-Americans, whether slave or free, were beginning to turn to Christianity. This would, in the course of time, have dire implications for the survival of slavery.

The Great Awakening performed a role in colonial America of great significance. It bound the people more closely than before with the bonds of a shared faith, a shared vision of the world that they inherited and in which they were destined to live. It thus contributed to the building of an American nationality that steeled Americans to face the ordeal of revolution and a war for independence when the time came.

AS OTHERS SEE US: America in 1750 Through the Eyes of Peter Kalm

About sixty years ago, the greatest part of this country was covered with tall and large trees, and the swamps were full of water. But it has undergone so great a change, as few other places have undergone in so short a time. At present the forests are cut down in most places, the swamps drained by ditches, the country cultivated, and changed into grain fields, meadows, and pastures.

Peter Kalm

When John Peter Zenger died in 1746, it was nearly 150 years since the first colonists had arrived in America. What changes had taken place in this span of time? How did the country look in 1750? How did the people live?

An answer to these questions is provided in the writing of Peter Kalm, a Swedish naturalist, who visited the colonies in 1748 and traveled extensively through the country before returning to Sweden in 1751. The publication of Kalm's *Travels in North America* began in 1753. Kalm was an eminent man who was welcomed everywhere and who talked to many people. As a scientist, he was a trained observer who paid attention to careful and accurate recording of detail. His work is an unrivaled source for the study of America's land and people at midcentury.

Peter Kalm arrived at Philadelphia on September 15, 1748. "The streets," he wrote, "run in a straight line and make right angles at the intersections...In most of the streets is a pavement of flagstones laid before the houses, and four-foot posts put on the outside. Those who walk on foot use the flat stones, but riders and teams use the middle of the street." The wooden posts gave pedestrians some security against careless teamsters and runaway horses. Nonetheless people who went on foot were in danger of being spattered by the dirt thrown up by the passing traffic. A gentleman, Kalm pointed out, when accompanying a lady, would always make sure that he was nearest the street and that she was on the inside, nearest the houses. "The custom," he said, "is supposed to have arisen from an attempt to protect the walking companion from the filth of the street; hence, the side next to it is held to be less honorable."

Kalm went on to enumerate the public buildings. Philadelphia had at this time no less than 12 churches. In some cases, the burying grounds were outside of town, in others in the churchyards, but "...the Negroes are buried in a separate place out of town." The other public buildings were the Town Hall, the Library, the Court House, and the Academy. The Town Hall, where the Assembly met, was noted Kalm, "...a fine, large building having a tower with a bell."

Philadelphia in 1750 was British America's capital city, its largest commercial center and its greatest port. Key to the town's prosperity was its location at the head of Delaware Bay. Even the biggest ocean-going vessels, Kalm noted, could sail right up the Delaware to the town and cast anchor in 25 feet of water.

The city conducted a thriving trade with other colonies, with England, Portugal and Latin America. To the West Indies, Kalm wrote, "the inhabitants ship almost every day a quantity of flour, butter, meat and other victuals, timber, planks and the like. In return they receive sugar, molasses, rum, indigo, mahogany." In return for the fine woods and other raw materials that they shipped to England, the Philadelphians brought back "all sorts of manufactured goods, that is, fine and coarse cloth, linen, ironware and other wrought metals."

By 1748, Philadelphia's trade was so extensive that 600 ships were entering and clearing port every year. The town was also a market center for the surrounding farm area. Every year, two great fairs were held, one in May, the other in November. In addition, every Wednesday and Saturday were market days, when "...the country people in Pennsylvania and New Jersey bring to town a quantity of food and other products of the country, and this is a great advantage to the town." During the very hot weather, added Kalm, there was a market nearly every day, "...for the victuals do not keep well in the great heat." The farm folk would arrive before dawn with their baskets and carts and take up their stands near the Court House. At about nine o'clock in the morning, or whenever their wares were sold, they would make their way back home to resume their labor in the fields.

Fisherfolk, too, sold their wares in town. Kalm noted the oystermen hawking their goods up and down the streets, uttering their special cries as they went. The waters of Philadelphia, in those days, were stocked with large and delicious oysters; from these, inhabitants made what we might call oysterburgers. "Philadelphians," said Kalm, "like to fry them on live coals until they begin to open. They are then eaten with a sandwich of soft wheat bread and butter."

Philadelphia had one disadvantage as a port, Kalm noted, and this was "...the freezing of the river almost every winter for a month or more. During this time, navigation is entirely stopped. This does not happen at Boston, New York, and other towns which are nearer the sea." The arrival of freezing weather was welcomed by the young people of the city, who had a passion for skating. Booths were set up on the ice for the sale of brandy and popcorn. "Sheltered spots," said Kalm, "were flooded with men skaters, but I saw no women on the ice here."

Kalm estimated the population of Philadelphia in 1750 as being considerably more than 10,000 souls. He was impressed by the city's "grandeur and perfection," and the speed of its growth. Pennsylvania, he said, "...was no better than a wilderness in the year 1681, and contained hardly fifteen hundred people; now it vies with several kingdoms of Europe in the number of its inhabitants."

On September 18, 1748, Kalm began to explore the countryside around Philadelphia. Cleared fields lay everywhere and in the midst of them were farmsteads. The farmhouses were built of brick or local stone; trees lined the paths leading from the houses to the highway. Eastern Pennsylvania farmers grew much grain; corn and buckwheat were everywhere. The corn, said Kalm "grew very well and to a great length, the stalks being from six to ten feet high and covered with fine green leaves." Fruit and nuts grew also in abundance. "Every countryman," he wrote, "even the poorest peasant, had an orchard with apples, peaches, chestnuts, walnuts, cherries, quinces and such fruits, and sometimes we saw vines climbing in them."

As for the highways of Pennsylvania, these were little more than grass-grown trails wandering through field and forest from farm to farm. Some roads that led over sandy soils and were, therefore, well-drained, were in good condition; others were quagmires. The people, Kalm observed, were careless about building bridges, and this made traveling dangerous. Travelers had to cross the streams as best they could, and many of them risked drowning when the waters rose after heavy rains.

Everywhere that Kalm went he saw tree stumps in fields only recently cleared for cultivation. The clearing of the forest in southeastern Pennsylvania had been accomplished in little more than 60 years, the time that had elapsed since the colony was founded during the 1680s. A great change was apparent. "The forests are cut down in most places," he wrote, "the swamps drained by ditches, the country cultivated, and turned into grain fields, meadows and pastures."

Kalm was one of the first travelers to describe the process by which the frontier farmer cleared the wilderness, mined the soil and moved ever westward in search of new and richer lands. "After the inhabitants have converted a tract of land into a tillable field," he wrote, "which has been a forest for many centuries, and which consequently has a very fine soil, the colonists use it as long as it will bear any crops; and when it ceases to bear any, they turn it into pastures for the cattle, and take new grain fields in another place, where a rich black soil can be found and where it has never been made use of."

This kind of farming, Kalm pointed out, could bring quick and easy riches for a few; in the long run, and for the country as a whole, it was a disaster. It resulted in the rapid destruction of deep and immensely rich forest soils, wiping out a resource that "had been spared by the fire or the ax ever since Creation," and converting it into mere pasture. This type of "hit and run" cultivation did no permanent damage when conducted on the puny scale practiced by the native Americans. When the continent began to be systematically ravaged in this way, it spelled the exhaustion of the land with all of its forest, mineral and wildlife riches. "Pioneer farmers," concluded Kalm, have "their eyes fixed on present gain, and they are blind to the future."

Here and there, he passed a little market town like Chester with stone or wooden houses, church and marketplace; once in a while he passed a forge.

About two English miles beyond Chester I passed by an iron forge, which was on the right by the roadside. It belonged to two brothers, as I was told. The ore however is not dug here but thirty or forty miles away, where it is first melted in a furnace and then carried to this place. The bellows were made of leather, and both they and the hammers, and even the hearth, were but small in proportion to ours. All the machines were worked by water. The iron was wrought into bars.

Kalm noticed everywhere, even as observers had a century and a half earlier, huge numbers of birds. "They fly in incredibly large flocks," he wrote, "and it can hardly be conceived whence such immense numbers of them can come. When they rise in the air they darken the sky, and make it look almost black."

He noted, too, a wealth of detail concerning the flowers and wildlife. The flying squirrels, in particular, intrigued him. "Among all the squirrels in this country," he wrote, "these are the most easily tamed. The boys carry them to school, or wherever they go, without their ever attempting to escape. Even if they put their squirrel aside, it leaps upon them again immediately, creeps either into their bosom or their sleeve, or any fold of the clothes, and lies down to sleep." More than 200 years later, in the 20th century, these squirrels would be far less numerous in America, but schoolchildren would still be taming them in the country districts and carrying them to school.

In 1750, men and women worked hard for their living, but the fertile soil yielded abundant harvests, which, wrote Kalm, "always afford plenty of bread for the inhabitants, though one year may be better than the rest." People could have honey as well as butter on their bread; bees were not native to North America but had been imported from England and did exceedingly well. Cake, wine and tea were served at wedding feasts, baptismal ceremonies and other social occasions.

Wine making was a common household chore for which all kinds of fruit, including the grape, were used. Said Kalm, "the ladies principally take white and red currants for that purpose, since the shrubs of this kind are very plentiful in the gardens and succeed very well. They likewise make a wine of strawberries, which grow in great plenty in the woods...Raspberries and cherries which are cultivated and well taken care of also give a fine wine."

In many parts of the country, cider was the farmer's everyday drink. It was made of apples and apple peelings boiled in water and fermented. "One who has not tasted it before," wrote Kalm, "would not believe that such a palatable beverage could be prepared from apples."

Buckwheat cakes were a favorite American food, both in the cities and the farm districts, for buckwheat was a general-purpose crop that thrived well on many types of soil, especially poor ones. Kalm tells us that "the cakes are usually made in the morning, and are baked in a frying pan or on a stone, are buttered and then eaten, when still warm, with tea or coffee, instead of toasted bread with butter, or toast, which the English usually eat at break-

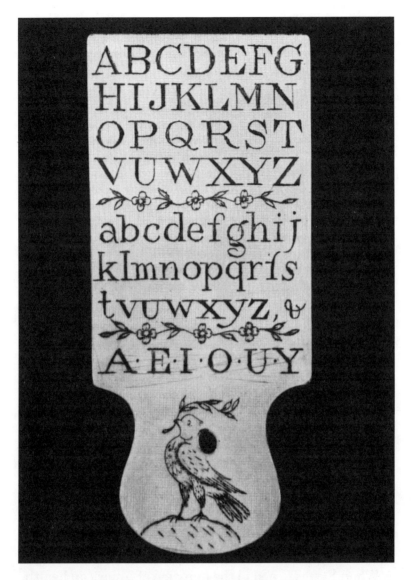

Children used "hornbooks" to learn the alphabet. To make one, a printed page was covered with a sheet of transparent horn. (Free Library of Philadelphia)

fast. The buckwheat cakes are very good, and are common at Philadelphia and in other English colonies, especially in winter."

Cheese, Kalm reported, was made and consumed on most American farms, but it varied very much in quality from place to place. His praise, however, of apple dumplings, a special favorite of colonists of British origin, was unqualified. Dough was prepared, rolled thin, and wrapped around the apple. Each dumpling was then bound up in a linen cloth and boiled in a pot; when the dumplings were cooked, says Kalm, rather quaintly, "...you get as many dumplings as you have apples."

The usual type of illumination for the evening meal and the long winter evenings was, among the common people, the open fire or the tallow candle made from the fat of the ox. In some parts of the country, bayberry candles were made and used on special occasions; sometimes a superior candle was made from a mixture of tallow and bayberry wax. Bayberry, wrote Kalm, "grows abundantly in wet soil, and it seems to thrive particularly well in the neighborhood of the sea...The berries...are gathered late in autumn...and are then thrown into a kettle or pot full of boiling water. By this means their fat melts out, floats at the top of the water, and is skimmed off into a vessel."

By 1750, sperm candles were also coming into use among the more well-to-do, for they were a luxury that cost four times as much as the ordinary tallow candles. Spermaceti, the raw material, was a special fat taken from the head of the whale. In the course of time, as whaling became a major American industry, more and more American homes would be illuminated with oil lamps, rather than with candles.

When Kalm turned to the question of American health, he did not paint so rosy a picture. He was puzzled by the fact that Americans of both sexes, but especially women, began to lose their teeth at an absurdly early age. "Girls," he wrote, "not above twenty years old frequently had lost half of their teeth without any hopes of getting new ones." No matter what their parentage was—Swedish, English, German, Dutch, or native-born—the story was the same. It was particularly puzzling in view of the fact that the

Indians seemed to be immune to this unpleasant affliction. "They live in the same air," said Kalm, "and always keep their teeth in a fine, white condition as long as they live." Kalm thought at first it might have something to do with tea, "which is drunk here in the morning and afternoon, especially by women, and is so common at present that there is hardly a farmer's wife or a poor woman who does not drink tea in the morning." But he had to abandon this theory when he met a group of young women who lost their teeth before they ever contracted the American habit of drinking tea.

Fever, which attacked many Americans and killed some, was a more serious handicap. Kalm wrote:

It generally begins with a headache followed by chills and fever. Often the chill is so great that both the patient, the bed upon which he lies, and everything else, shakes violently...No age is safe against it. In those places where it rages annually you see old men and women attacked by it, and even children in the cradle, sometimes not above three weeks old.

Kalm noted that the fever might rage in parts of the country, and that in other areas hardly a person might be afflicted. The causes of malaria were not known at that time, but Kalm gave a graphic description of the culprit. "The gnats, he wrote, "come into the houses, and when the people have gone to bed they begin their disagreeable humming, approaching nearer and nearer to the bed, and at last suck up so much blood that they can hardly fly away." When the weather cooled, the mosquitoes vanished, but after rain they swarmed in enormous numbers. "In the greatest heat of summer," he wrote, "they are so numerous in some places that the air seems to be full of them, especially near swamps and stagnant waters."

By 1750, the American population had reached more than 3.5 million, including about 750,000 slaves. Infant mortality was high, but families were large. The reason for this seemed clear enough. "As soon," Kalm said, "as a person is old enough he may marry in these provinces without any fear of poverty. There is such an amount of good land yet uncultivated that a newly married man can, without difficulty, get a spot of ground where he may comfortably subsist with his wife and children. The taxes are very low, and he need not be under any concern on that account."

The American colonists were highly articulate: they expressed their ideas about the beauty of their land, the sorrows they encountered, the opportunities they found and the struggles they fought in vivid and even glowing language. Their written words are preserved for us in letters, files, archives and books and are part of our heritage. But the colonists did not only talk and write about their lives and experiences—they sang of these things, too. A human message transmitted through song is a magnificent part of this heritage.

10

THE SYCAMORE TREE:
Songs the People Sang

Oh, have you come with silver and gold
And money to buy me free;
Or have you come to see me hung
Upon the sycamore tree?

The Sycamore Tree

The settlers who came here from across the Atlantic brought with them a marvelous but invisible baggage in the songs that they had learned and sung in the Old World. Many of these songs were hundreds of years old even when the European settlement of America began; they enshrined the stories and the legends of the people of Great Britain. Such songs, that do not only express a mood, but also tell a tale, we call ballads.

One of the loveliest of these British ballads is "The Gypsy Laddie"; it is a "borderland ballad" from the region of the Scots-English border northwest of the Cheviot Hills. The song tells of a nobleman's wife who gave up everything to follow her gypsy lover: it has been set to many melodies, but the one given here is among the oldest. For 300 years or more, this has been one of the first songs that many a British and American child has learned. It has been found in every state of the Union from Maine to Texas.

The Gypsy Laddie
(GYPSY DAVY)

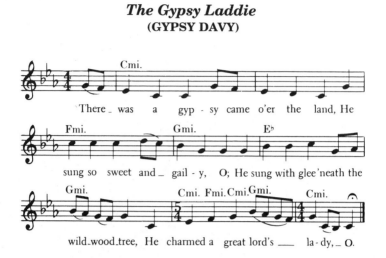

"Go bring me down my high-heeled shoes,
    All made of Spanish leather, O;
And I'll put on my Lowland brogues,
    To trip it o'er the heather, O."

The lord he came home late that night,
    Enquiring for his lady, O; "She's gone,
she's gone," said the old servant man,
    "She's gone with the gypsy Davy, O."

"Go saddle me my best black mare;
    The grey is ne'er so speedy, O;
For I'll ride all night, and I'll ride all day,
    Til I overtake my lady, O."

Riding down by the riverside,
    The grass was wet and dewy, O;
Seated with her gypsy lad,
    It's there he spied his lady, O.

"Will you forsake your house and home,
    Will you forsake you baby, O?
Will you forsake your own true love,
    And go with the gypsy Davy, O?"

(The melody lines of all songs included are chorded for guitar.)

"Yes, I'll forsake my house and home,
  Yes, I'll forsake my baby, O;
And I'll forsake my own true love,
  To go with the gypsy Davy, O.

"Last night I lay on a goose-feather bed,
  Sheets turned down so bravely, O;
To-night I'll lie in the mud and the rain,
  By the side of the gypsy Davy, O."

The lyric given here is from New England. The melody is English
traditional.

Another old ballad that rivaled "The Gypsy Laddie" in
popularity with the early settlers was called "The Maid
Freed from the Gallows," or, as it became known in America,"The Sycamore Tree." We reproduce it here because,
like the "Gypsy Laddie," it was one of the traditional songs
that children learned soonest and loved best. From the
earliest times, generations of American children, all over
this wide land, have danced and skipped to the rhythms
of this song.

"The Sycamore Tree's" popularity was due not only to
the vitality and beauty of the various melodies to which
it was sung, but also to its message. A human being, it
says, may be abandoned by all the world but can still live
if just one person loves him truly. The lyric is also of
interest from a historical point of view. We must not
conclude that because a person found himself on the
gallows he was necessarily particularly wicked. In the
16th and 17th centuries, a poor and hungry person in
Europe might be hanged for the smallest offense—even
for stealing a loaf of bread. It was just such people,
fleeing from starvation, injustice and the gallows, who
came to settle America.

The song also expresses a truth that was to become
as familiar to Americans as it was to Europeans.
People with money can buy their way out of almost
any scrape.

The Sycamore Tree

"Oh, hang - man, hang - man, slack - en your rope, And
wait a lit - tle while; — I think I see my
fa - ther com - ing, A - rid - ing from man - y a
mile." _____ "Oh, have you come — with
sil - ver and gold — And mon - ey to buy me
free, ___ Or have you come to see me hung Up -
on the syc - a - more tree?" _____ "No
gold nor sil - ver have ___ I here, Nor
mon - ey to buy — you free; — But I have come to

see ___ you hang Up - on   the syc - a - more tree."___

Repeat with mother, brother, sister and finally lover, who reply:

"Yes gold and silver have I here,
And money to buy you free;
But I've not come to see you hang
Nor hung you shall not be."

In colonial America, few settlers were very far from the ocean or from one of the great rivers flowing into it. The sea was the colonists' main gateway to the outside world; the ships that sailed on it carried colonial wares to Europe and the Caribbean and brought British news, literature and fashions to American doors. Thus, American lives and fortunes were bound up inextricably with the sea.

The ocean was a source of danger as well as profit. Many of the coasts that it washed were wild and uncharted; hidden rocks and unmarked reefs abounded; port channels were neither dredged nor blazed. Ships ran aground, were pounded to pieces on the headlands or were engulfed in storms. Block Island alone, at the mouth of Long Island Sound, was the scene of hundreds of major wrecks during the colonial era.

Naturally enough, therefore, many old ballads dealt with tragedy at sea; it is understandable that such songs were popular with the colonial people. One of the loveliest of these sea ballads is "The Lowlands of Holland." Composed in Britain some time during the 18th century, in one form or another it soon became popular in the New World.

The Lowlands of Holland

The   love   that   I ___   have   cho - sen,   I'll

there - with be con - tent, The salt sea shall _ be
fro - zen Be - fore I do _ re - pent; Re -
pent it shall _ I nev - er Un - til the day I
die, And the rag - ing sea and the
storm - y winds Have par - ted my love _ and me.

My love lies in the salt sea
   And I am on the side,
Enough to break a young thing's heart
   Who lately was a bride;
Who lately was a bonny bride
   With pleasure in her eye,
But the raging sea and the stormy winds
   Have parted my love and me

My love he built a gallant ship,
   A ship of noted fame
With four and twenty seamen bold
   To box her about the main;
To box her about the main, my boys
   Without a fear or doubt,
'Twas then my love and his gallant ship
   Were sorely tossed about.

"Oh daughter, dearest daughter,
　What makes you so lament,
Is there never a man in all our town
　Can give your heart content?"
"There is no lad in all our town,
　No lord nor duke for me,
I never never had but one true love,
　And he was drowned at sea,"

"There shall no mantle cross my back,
　Nor comb go in my hair,
Neither shall coal nor candlelight
　Shine in my bower more.
Nor shall I choose another love
　Until the day I die,
For I never had but one true love,
　And he was drowned at sea."

The lyric as given here was published in Scotland in 1788. The
melody is traditional.

No song in the English-American tradition has been
more widely sung, with more endless variations, than
"Waly Waly." No more deeply personal lament has come
down to us; none, certainly, that has fashioned the English
language in words more simple, expressive and moving.
In one sense, *Waly* is an invocation to the western wind—
that surging autumnal gale that roars through the trees,
moans under the doors and rattles the window panes.
These winds have figured frequently in English poetry. A
famous medieval fragment asks:

Westron wynde, when wilt thou blow?
The small rayne down can rayne.
Cryst, if my love were in my armys
And I in my bed again.

And in the 20th century, an English poet, James Elroy
Flecker, speaks of:

queer winds like Harlequins
That seized our elms for violins,
And struck a note so sharp and low
Even a child could feel its woe.

Waly, Waly

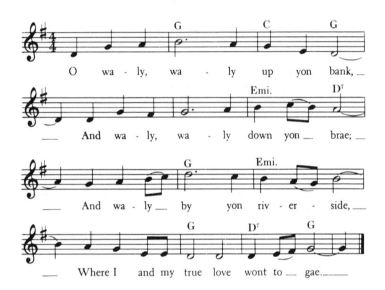

O waly, waly, up yon bank, —
And waly, waly, down yon — brae; —
And waly — by yon river - side, —
Where I and my true love wont to — gae.——

I leaned my back against an oak,
Thinking it was a trusty tree;
But first it bowed, and then it broke,
And so did my false love to me.

O waly, waly, love is bonny,
A little while when it is new;
But when 'tis old, it waxes cold,
And fades away like morning dew.

When cockle shells turn silver bells,
And mussels grow on every tree;
When frost and snow shall warm us all,
Then shall my love prove true to me.

O western wind, when wilt thou blow,
And shake the green leaves off the tree,
O gentle death, when wilt thou come,
And take a life that wearies me?

But had I wist before I kissed,
That love had been so ill to win,
I'd have locked my heart in a case of gold,
And pinned it up with a silver pin.

I wish I wish my babe were born,
And smiling on its daddy's knee,
And I to be in yon church yard,
For a maid again I'll never be.

gae = go;
brae = valley;
waxes = grows;
wist = known.

"Hush, Little Baby" one of America's favorite cradle songs, seems to have originated in Alabama, but it is safe to say that something very like it was sung during colonial times. Generations of American children have been hushed to sleep with this song. Along with it, we reproduce an Irish lullaby, "The Castle of Dromore." This is perhaps one of the most beautiful of all the melodies that Irish immigrants brought with them to these shores. Irish songs are quite different from the British in mood, content and style. Irish settlers were coming to the colonies in the late 17th century; over the years, the trickle would turn into a flood. Irish-Americans would make a contribution to American singing second to none.

Hush, Little Baby

Hush, lit - tle ba - by,   don't   say   a   word,

Pa - pa's gon - na   buy   you   a   mock - ing   bird.

If that mocking bird won't sing,
Papa's gonna buy you a diamond ring.

If that diamond ring turns brass,
Papa's gonna buy you a looking glass.

If that looking glass gets broke,
Papa's gonna buy you a billy goat.

If that billy goat won't pull,
Papa's gonna buy you a cart and bull.

If that cart and bull turn over,
Papa's gonna buy you a dog named
    Rover.

If that dog named Rover won't bark,
Papa's gonna buy you a horse and cart.

If that horse and cart fall down,
You'll still be the sweetest little baby in
    town

Hush, little baby, don't say a word,
Papa's gonna buy you a mocking bird.

A 17th-century doll's cradle.
(New Hampshire Historical Society)

The Castle of Dromore

241 Oc - to - ber winds la - ment a - round _ the cas - tle of Dro - more; ___ But _ peace is in her loft - y halls, __ my dear - est treas - ure store. ___ Though _ au - tumn leaves __ may droop __ and die, a bud of spring __ are you, _____ Sing - ing hush - a - bye, lull - a - bye, lou lo lan, Sing hush - a - bye, lou lo lan. (Hum) _____

The children of colonial America had dozens of singing games to enliven their play. A number of these—like "London Bridge Is Falling Down," and "Here We Go Round the Mulberry Bush"—are still in circulation. "Lazy John," reproduced below, was very popular with children in the old days, and is still sung by them in certain parts of the country. It is followed by the all-time children's favorite, "Let's Go a-Huntin!" The British original of this ditty dates back five centuries or more; American children have been singing their own versions from the very earliest days.

Lazy John

[Continue as above, substituting in turn the following items of clothing: coat, shirt, pants, stockings, shoes and any other items that you can think of. When you are tired, end as follows:]

"Lazy John, lazy John, will you marry me?
   Will you marry me?
"How can I marry you? With a wife and
   three children at home."

Let's Go A-Huntin'

Let's go a-hunt-in', said Risk-y Rob,
Let's go a-hunt-in', said Rob-in ___ to Bob,
Let's go a-hunt-in', said Dan'-l to Jo,
Let's go a-hunt-in', said Bil-ly Bar-low.

What shall we hunt for? said Risky Rob,
What shall we hunt for? said Robin to Bob,
What shall we hunt for? said Dan'l to Jo,
   Let's hunt for a rat, said Billy Barlow.

How shall we kill him? said Risky Rob,
How shall we kill him? said Robin to Bob,
How shall we kill him? said Dan'l to Jo,
   Borrow a gun, said Billy Barlow.

How shall we haul him? said, Risky Rob,
How shall we haul him? said Robin to Bob,
How shall we haul him? said Dan'l to Jo,
   Borrow a cart, said Billy Barlow.

How shall we divide him? said Risky Rob,
How shall we divide him? said Robin to Bob,
How shall we divide him? said Dan'l to Jo,
    Borrow a knife, said Billy Barlow.

How shall we cook him? said Risky Rob,
How shall we cook him? said Robin to Bob,
How shall we cook him? said Dan'l to Jo,
    Over a fire, said Billy Barlow.

I'll roast shoulder, said Risky Rob,
I'll boil legs, said Robin to Bob,
I'll bake back, said Dan'l to Jo,
    Tail bone raw, said Billy Barlow.

I feel sick, said Risky Rob,
I gotta bellyache, said Robin to Bob,
OOOOOOps!! said Dan'l to Jo,
    I feel fine, said Billy Barlow.

"The Old Man Who Lived in the Woods" is a colonial ballad that was well loved and widely sung throughout British America. The verses in this amusing tale give us a vivid idea of some of the chores that fell to a woman on the average pioneer farm—washing dirty laundry, milking the cow, churning the cream, feeding the animals, spinning and winding yarn. Woman's work was never done; were there not also children to bear and to mind, meals to cook and floors to scrub?

The Old Man Who Lived in the Woods

There was an old man who lived in the woods, As you shall plain-ly see, Who said he could do more

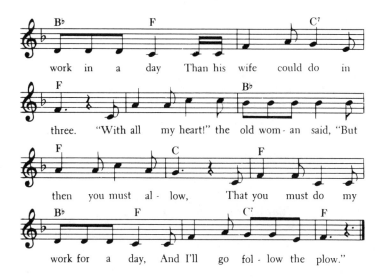

work in a day Than his wife could do in
three. "With all my heart!" the old wom-an said, "But
then you must al - low, That you must do my
work for a day, And I'll go fol - low the plow."

"You must milk the tiny cow,
  Lest she should go quite dry,
And you must feed the little pigs
  That live in yonder sty.

"You must watch the speckled hen,
  For fear she lays astray,
And not forget the spool of yarn
  That I spin every day."

The old woman took the staff in her hand,
  And went to follow the plow;
And the old man took the pail on his head
  And went to milk the cow.

But Tiny she winked and Tiny she blinked,
  And Tiny she tossed her nose,
And Tiny she gave him a kick on the shins
  Till the blood ran down to his toes.

Then "Whoa, Tiny!" and "So, Tiny!
  My pretty little cow, stand still!
If ever I milk you again," he said,
  "It will be against my will."

And then he went to feed the pigs
  That lived within the sty;
The old sow ran against his legs
  And threw him in the mire.

And then he watched the speckled hen
  Lest she might lay astray;
But he quite forgot the spool of yarn
  That his wife spun every day.

Then the old man swore by the sun and
    the moon,
  And the green leaves on the trees,
That his wife could do more work in a day
  Than he could do in three.

And when he saw how well she plowed,
  And ran the furrows even,
He swore she could do more work in a day
  Than he could do in seven.

CONCLUSION

British explorers laid claim to North America on behalf of their sovereign, the king of England. He, in turn, granted rights of ownership and exploitation to chartered companies composed of noblemen and merchants, and to high-born proprietors. The settlement of the New World was organized by this leadership, motivated by the hope of private fortune and personal gain. New England communities in Massachusetts, Connecticut and Rhode Island provided the main exception to this rule.

Colonists crossed the Atlantic for many reasons but above all to escape the sadness, bitterness and poverty of life in the Old World. In some cases, they were lured by promises and propaganda. Others were kidnapped and taken by main force or came as prisoners of war. Some were felons who preferred the perils of exile to the penalty of execution for stealing a sheep. Many died in passage; the survivors found their home in a land of unbelievable beauty, fertility and extent.

America was peopled by scattered tribes of Indians who lived partly from fishing, food gathering and the hunt, and partly from the cultivation of corn and vegetables in their forest clearings. The white man possessed a technology in advance of the stone tools of these neolithic people; he knew the use of firearms, the plough and the ax. He killed the native peoples, drove them away or enslaved them. They cleared the forests, planted farms, built ships and developed a wide-ranging commerce with the world beyond the seas. The wealthier farmers, particularly in the South, soon found that the labor of white servants was inadequate for their needs. They began to import black slaves from Africa.

By 1750, 13 mainland colonies had come into existence; their control extended the length and breadth of British America—from the Atlantic to the Appalachians, from Maine to Georgia. Most of them, by this time, were royal colonies, directly under the rule of the king and of governors appointed by him. All possessed assemblies, to some extent elected by and representative of the general population. But the community in every case was stratified. New England was a land of small farmers, craftspeople, and fisherfolk dominated by a merchant leadership whose wealth came from the fisheries, the slave trade and seaborne commerce with Europe and the West Indies. Large landowners and wealthy merchants, in the same way, provided the leadership of New York and Pennsylvania. As for the South, it was almost completely an agricultural region ruled by a coterie of wealthy planters who owned huge tracts of land and raised crops with slave labor primarily for export to the European market.

By 1750, there was a sharp differentiation between the mass of ordinary American settlers and the merchant-planter aristocracy. But many factors, too, operated to bind all Americans together with a common consciousness of an American nationality with its own identity and special interests. The people lived in a land that they cleared with their own sweat and blood; it was a land set apart from other lands, a unique and special possession of those that inhabited it, cultivated it, and loved it. These people spoke the same language, lived under the same law, shared the same memories of the past, enjoyed the same literature and sang the same songs. They faced the same enemies, fought for the same goals and shared a common destiny. They based their philosophy of life on the same creed, and they worshipped the same God.

During these years, the colonial people fashioned an economic, political and social structure that was to provide the foundations for American civilization.

BIBLIOGRAPHY

CHAPTER 1   WANDERERS IN EDEN
Sefan Lorant, ed., *The New World: the First Pictures of America* (New York: Duell, Sloan and Pearce, 1946), includes a number of early narratives with descriptions of Indian life, also reproductions of the watercolors that John White made in Virginia, 1585–87. The anthology compiled by T.C. McLuhan, *Touch the Earth: A Self-Portrait of Indian Existence* (New York: Outerbridge and Dienstfrey, distributed by E.P. Dutton & Co., 1971) is an anthology in which native American people themselves express their philosophy and their feelings. It is illustrated with portraits from the Edward S. Curtis photographic collection worthy of Rembrandt. Alvin M. Josephy, Jr., *The Indian Heritage of America* (New York: Alfred A. Knopf, 1968); and the Editors of American Heritage, *The American Heritage Book of Indians* (New York: American Heritage Publishing Co., distributed by Simon and Schuster, Inc., 1961), are admirable surveys of the civilization of indigenous American peoples. The second of these two books has fine maps and illustrations. Numerous writings testifying to the nature and beauty of America on the arrival of the white people are scattered through J. Franklin Jameson, ed., *Original Narratives of Early American History* (New York: Charles Scribner; 1909–15: reprinted by Barnes and Noble, 1959–66). Robert Beverly's *History and Present State of Virginia* (1705) is available in a modern edition

prepared by Louis B. Wright (Chapel Hill: University of North Carolina Press, 1947). For John Lederer's story see William P. Cumming, ed., *The Discoveries of John Lederer* (Charlottesville: University of Virginia Press, 1958).

CHAPTER 2   THE WEATHERBEATEN SHORE: *Early Settlers in New England.*

Samuel Eliot Morison has issued a definitive edition of William Bradford's *Of Plymouth Plantation 1620–47* (New York: Alfred A. Knopf, 1952). Thomas Dudley, "Letter to Bridget, Countess of Lincoln," is reproduced in John Anthony Scott, ed., *Living Documents in American History*, vol. 1 (New York: Washington Square Press, 1964). For a vivid picture of the lives of the early Massachusetts settlers, see Darrett B. Rutman, *Husbandmen of Plymouth: Farms and Villages in the Old Colony, 1620–92* (Boston: published by Beacon Press for Plimoth Plantation, 1967). Carl Bridenbaugh, *Cities in the Wilderness: the First Century of Urban Life* (New York: Alfred A. Knopf, 1964), deals with the development of Boston.

CHAPTER 3   THE CAPTIVITY OF MARY ROWLANDSON

Mary Rowlandson's *Narrative* is reproduced in Charles H. Lincoln, ed., *Narratives of the Indian Wars 1675–99* (New York: Barnes and Noble, 1959); also in Richard Slotkin and James K. F. Folsom, eds.,*So Dreadful a Judgment: Puritan Responses to King Philip's War 1676–7* (Middletown, CT: Wesleyan University Press, 1978). Background for King Philip's war is provided by Alden T. Vaughan, *New England Frontier: Puritans and Indians, 1620–75* (Boston: Little, Brown, 1965). See Alvin Josephy, *The Patriot Chiefs, A Chronicle of American Indian Leadership* (New York: The Viking Press, 1961), for a chapter on King Philip and an overview of the war. Douglas Edward Leach, *Flintlock and Tomahawk: New England in King Philip's War* (New York: W. W. Norton, 1966), unfolds the struggle in greater detail.

CHAPTER 4   THE WOODS OF WILLIAM PENN AND HOW THEY WERE SETTLED

Gottlieb Mittelberger, *Journey to Pennsylvania*, is available in a modern version edited and translated by Oscar Handlin and John L. Clive (Cambridge: The Belknap Press of Harvard University Press, 1960). Additional documentary materials for the early history of Pennsylvania are to be found in Albert C. Myers, ed., *Narratives of Early Pennsylvania, West New Jersey, and Delaware: 1630–1707* (New York: Barnes and Noble, 1959). For Philadelphia see Carl Bridenbaugh, *Cities in the Wilderness 1625–1742*, cited above; and Frederick B. Tolles, *Meeting House and Counting House: the Quaker Merchants of Colonial Philadelphia 1682–1783* (New York: W. W. Norton, 1963). Detailed studies of immigrant labor in colonial America include David Galenson, *White Servitude in Colonial America: An Economic Analysis* (New York: Cambridge University Press, 1981); Abbot E. Smith, *Colonists in Bondage: White Servants and Convict Labor in America 1607–1776* (Raleigh: University of North Carolina Press, 1947); and A. Roger Ekirch, *Bound for America: the Transportation of British Convicts to the Colonies, 1718–75* (New York: Oxford University Press, 1987). Settlement of Pennsylvania farmlands is the subject of a fine study by James T. Lemon, *The Best Poor Man's Country: A Geographical Study of Early Southeastern Pennsylvania* (Baltimore: The Johns Hopkins Press, 1972).

CHAPTER 5   OUTPOST OF EMPIRE: *Virginia and Its Planters in the 17th Century*

Sources indispensable for 17th-century Virginia are Lyon Gardiner Taylor, ed., *Narratives of Early Virginia*, and Charles M. Andrews, ed., *Narratives of the Insurrections, 1675–90* (New York: Barnes and Noble, 1966 and 1959 respectively). Edmund S. Morgan, *American Slavery American Freedom: the Ordeal of Colonial Virginia*, (New York: W. W. Norton, 1975), is a major contribution. Sources for Bacon's Rebellion are provided in Wilcomb E. Washburn, *The Governor and the Rebel* (Chapel Hill: University of North Carolina Press, 1957).

CHAPTER 6   THE BLACK FOUNDATION: *Bringing Africans to the New World*
Elizabeth Donnan, *Documents Illustrative of the History of the Slave Trade to America* is a basic source (originally published in 1930 in 4 vols.; reprinted New York: Octagon Books, 1965). John Hope Franklin, *From Slavery to Freedom: A History of American Negroes* (New York: Alfred A. Knopf, 2d ed., 1963), provides an overview, pages 3–110. See also Basil Davidson's *Black Mother, the Years of the African Slave Trade* (Boston: Little, Brown, 1961); Daniel P. Mannix and Malcolm Cowley, *Black Cargoes, a History of the African Slave Trade* (New York: The Viking Press, 1962); and Jay Coughtry, *The Notorious Triangle: Rhode Island and the African Slave Trade, 1700–1807* (Philadelphia: Temple University Press, 1981). Philip D. Curtin, *The Atlantic Slave Trade, A Census* (Madison: University of Wisconsin Press, 1968), sets forth a realistic estimate of the number of Africans imported to the New World between 1451 and 1870. For black struggle against slavery in the colonial South, see Gerald W. Mullin, *Flight and Rebellion: Slave Resistance in Eighteenth-Century Virginia* (New York: Oxford University Press, 1972); and Peter H. Wood, *Black Majority: Negroes in Colonial South Carolina from 1670 through the Stono Rebellion [1739]* (New York: W. W. Norton, 1974).

CHAPTER 7   MARTYR IN MANHATTAN: *Governor Cosby and the Trial of John Peter Zenger*
Documentary material on the history of New York is available in J. Franklin Jameson, ed., *Narratives of New Netherlands 1609–1664*, and *The Journal of Jasper Danckaerts 1679–80* (New York: Barnes and Noble, 1959). See also Jerome Rich, *Jacob Leisler's Rebellion: A Study of Democracy in New York, 1664–1720* (Chicago: University of Chicago Press, 1953); and Carl Bridenbaugh, *Cities in the Wilderness*, cited above. Livingston Rutherfurd published James Alexander's report of Zenger's trial in 1904 under the title *John Peter Zenger: His Press, His Trial* (reissued New York: Peter Smith, 1941). A more recent edition, with supplementary material, is Stanley

Nizer Katz, ed., *Brief Narrative of the Case and Trial of John Peter Zenger, by James Alexander* (Cambridge: Harvard University Press, 1972). Leonard W. Levy, in *The Emergence of a Free Press* (New York: Oxford University Press, 1985) summarizes the Zenger case in Chapter 2 and has commentary in Chapter 5. The treatment is provocative but not adequately elaborated.

CHAPTER 8   THE FOUR WINDS: *Jonathan Edwards and the Great Awakening*
Nathan Cole's account of the Middletown, Connecticut meeting of October 1740, taken from his unpublished autobiography, is reproduced in Allen Heimert and Perry Miller, eds., *The Great Awakening: Documents Illustrating the Crisis and its Consequences* (New York: The Bobbs-Merrill Co., 1967). George Whitefield's *Journals* (London: Banner of Truth Trust, 1960), are available from the Bible Truth Depot, Swengel, Pennsylvania. Ola Elizabeth Winslow, ed., *Jonathan Edwards: Basic Writings* (New York: New American Library, 1966), is an excellent selection. The exquisite account of Abigail Hutchinson from the *Faithful Narrative of the Surprising Works of God...* is found in John Anthony Scott, ed., *Living Documents in American History* (New York: Washington Square Press, 1963), Vol. 1, 115–24. "Sinners in the Hands of an Angry God," and Charles Chauncy's "Letter from a Gentleman in Boston" are reproduced at the same place, page 124 ff. There are biographies of Edwards by Ola E. Winslow (New York: Collier Books, 1961), and by Perry Miller (New York: Meridian Books, 1959).

CHAPTER 9   AS OTHERS SEE US: *America in 1750 Through the Eyes of Peter Kalm*
This chapter is based on Peter Kalm, *Travels in North America*, revised and edited by Adolph Benson from the English version of 1770 (New York: Dover Publications, 1966, 2 vols.). This is a charming source for those interested in the life and the environment of the American people in colonial times.

CHAPTER 10   THE SYCAMORE TREE: *Songs the People Sang*
Francis James Child, *The English and Scottish Popular Ballads* (New York: Pageant Book Company, 5 vols.); Bertrand Harris Bronson, *The Traditional Tunes of the Child Ballads* (Princeton: Princeton University Press, 1959–72, 4 vols.); and Donal O'Sullivan, ed., *Songs of the Irish* (New York: Crown Publishers, 1960), are fundamental references for the British-American song heritage. John Anthony Scott, *The Ballad of America* (Carbondale: Southern Illinois University Press, 1983, 2d ed., revised), makes available a number of colonial songs with music, commentary and discography. Many more are found in John Jacob Niles, *The Ballad Book* (New York: Bramhall House, 1960); Eloise Hubbard Linscott, *Folk Songs of Old New England* (Hamden, Connecticut: The Shoe String Press, 1962); and Cecil Sharp, *English Folk Songs from the Southern Appalachians* (New York: Oxford University Press, 1960. Edited by Maude Karpeles).

ACKNOWLEDGMENTS

Grateful acknowledgment is made for permission to excerpt from the following works:

Journey to Pennsylvania by Gottlieb Mittleberger, edited and translated by Oscar Handlin and John Clive. Copyright 1960 by the President and Fellows of Harvard College, Harvard University Press, Cambridge, Mass.

Of Plymouth Plantation by William Bradford, edited by Samuel Eliot Morison. Published, 1952, by Alfred A. Knopf, Inc. Reprinted by permission of the publisher.

Peter Kalm's Travels in North America, revised and edited by Adolph B. Benson. Copyright 1966 by Dover Publications, Inc., New York. Reprinted by permission of the publisher.

The Discoveries of John Lederer, edited by William P. Cumming. Copyright 1958 by the University of Virginia Press. Reprinted by permission of the publisher.

INDEX

JOHN ANTHONY SCOTT holds degrees in history from Oxford and Columbia Universities. He has taught at Columbia University, Amherst College, the Ethical Culture Schools in New York City and Rutgers University School of Law. Scott is the author or editor of many books, including *Woman Against Slavery: the Story of Harriet Beecher Stowe*, *Teaching for a Change*, and *John Brown of Harper's Ferry*. A long time critic of the mediocre texts that secondary school students are obliged to use in their classes, he has called for the replacement of these books by writing endowed by vitality and good scholarship.